The Ground and ~~Grammar~~

O F

THEOLOGY

The Ground and Grammar

O F

THEOLOGY

Consonance between Theology and Science

Thomas F. Torrance

T&T CLARK
EDINBURGH & NEW YORK

T&T CLARK LTD

A Continuum imprint

59 George Street
Edinburgh EH2 2LQ
Scotland

www.tandtclark.co.uk

370 Lexington Avenue
New York 10017–6503
USA

www.continuumbooks.com

First published 1980 by University Press of Virginia
and Christian Journals Limited, Belfast

First published in paperback 2001 by T&T Clark Ltd

ISBN 0 567 08778 6

British Library Cataloguing-in-Publication Data
A catalogue record for this book is available from the British Library

British Library Cataloguing-in-Publication Data
A catalogue record for this book is available from the British Library

Contents

Preface to the New Edition vii

Preface ix

1. Man, the Priest of Creation   1

2. Emerging from the Cultural Split 15

3. Creation and Science 44

4. The Transformation of Natural Theology 75

5. Theological Science 110

6. The Basic Grammar of Theology 146

Index of Names 179

TO

John Marks Templeton

in high regard and deep admiration

Preface to the
New Edition

THIS BOOK WAS FIRST published by the University Press of Virginia in 1980 in which I was concerned to bring to light some of the important connections between Christian Theology and Natural Science. In it I sought to clarify the relations of Christian theology to the two great dualist cosmologies of the past, the Ptolemaic and Copernican-Newtonian, and to the non-dualist cosmological outlook arising out of the radical change in the basic rationality of science which we owe to Einstein, and, as he claimed, to James Clerk Maxwell. In it I did not point to the work of Clerk Maxwell, which I have discussed elsewhere: particularly in the book *Transformation and Convergence in the Frame of Knowledge*, published by Christian Journals Limited of Belfast (which also published an edition of this work in 1980), and in my edition of his epoch-making book *A Dynamical Theory of the Electromagnetic Field*, Edinburgh 1982, now published by Wipf & Stock, Eugene, Oregon. Two of the reasons for reissuing *The Ground and Grammar of Theology* now are my attempt in it to clarify the trinitarian structure of Christian theology, and the discussion that has been raised by the transformation of so-called natural theology. Unfortunately the chapter entitled "The Transformation of Natural Theology" has been seriously misunderstood by a number of people who use it to support and justify their own unreconstructed conceptions of "natural theology". May I direct them to Chapter 5 of my book *Karl Barth, Biblical and Evangelical Theologian*, published by T&T Clark in 1990?

This book, like the original edition, is dedicated to John Marks Templeton, in high regard and deep admiration.

Advent, 2000   T.F.T.
Edinburgh

Preface

A FULLER TITLE FOR THESE LECTURES more explicitly related to what they are intended to be about, would
be "The Ground and Grammar of a Realist Theology in
the ·Perspective of a Unitary Understanding of the Creation." I believe that human thought is now in the midst of
one of the greatest transitions of history, which we must
take with the utmost seriousness—a transition away from
cosmological and epistemological dualisms that have had,
as we now realize, a damaging effect on human culture, in
science and philosophy, and not least upon religion and theology. Throughout the lectures (or chapters as they now
are), I keep asking what happens when we move from a
dualist outlook to a unitary outlook, and to the realist
modes of thought that arise in such an outlook, in which
we have restored to us the unity of form and being. The
dualist outlook that we have to transcend here affects not
only our intramundane relations but our understanding of
the relation between God and the created universe, for they
are mutually affected by each other. Conversely, a unitary
outlook upon the created universe and the doctrine of God
as the one creative Source of all order in the universe are
profoundly interconnected. Hence, fundamental to all that
follows are the Christian doctrine of God, the Creator and
Redeemer, and the doctrine of the creation itself, within
which God reveals himself to us and within which man, as
man of science and man of faith, is called to be the priest of

creation. That is the context in which all theological understanding unfolds and takes shape, but it is a context in
which theological science and natural science are found to
overlap with one another at profound points. This calls for
some far-reaching changes in traditional theology; but it
does mean that theology becomes properly established on
its own ontological ground, and its intrinsic structure is
correspondingly clarified and developed.

In the first chapter I seek to offer a brief account of the
changed perspective in science and theology and the promise of a new kind of synthesis, which incorporates the address I delivered on receiving the Templeton Foundation
Prize for Progress in Religion in March 1978. In the second
chapter I discuss the underlying ground of dualism which
has so deeply affected historic and modern thought, and
which needs to be understood clearly, since it lies at the
root of our present problems in the split culture, evident
not only in the regrettable hiatus between the sciences and
the humanities but in the disintegration of form in the arts
and the strange regress into pluralism and polymorphism
in our social and cultural life—and even into what one may
well call a covert polytheism. But our real concern here is
more positive, with the breaking down of these dualisms in
a switch to a unitary (but non-monist) and realist outlook in
science and in theology. The deep integration of thought
that this involves is traced in the third chapter to certain
masterful conceptions basic to both science and theology,
which developed out of classical Christian theology as it
sought to think through the relation between the incarnation and the creation of space and time within which that
theology took place. The question is then asked, in the
fourth chapter, What happens to traditional natural theology, which has always flourished in periods of dualist and

deist modes of thought, when it seemed imperative to find some way of throwing a logical bridge across the gap between the world and God? In the transition to a unitary outlook, natural theology suffers a radical transformation much like that suffered by geometry in its assimilation as a four-dimensional natural science into the material content of physics and astrophysics. In the last two chapters I turn more explicitly to the modes and structures of thought that are developed in theological science as it becomes liberated from the tyranny of pseudo-scientific concepts and is pursued on its own proper ground, while in continuous dialogue with natural science in its deeper and more comprehensive understanding of the contingent universe. In the fifth chapter this is done with reference to three intriguing sayings of Einstein, when we find illuminating parallels, but also divergences, naturally cropping up between theological and natural science. In the final chapter I examine the stratified structure of such a theology, as it becomes apparent in the course of inquiry that presses into the ultimate ground of intelligible relations in God himself, when the doctrine of the Trinity is found to constitute the ultimate unitary basis on which a clarification and simplification of all theology may be carried out. Thus it is finally in our understanding of the trinitarian relations in God himself that we have the ground and grammar of a realist theology.

I WOULD LIKE TO EXPRESS MY GRATITUDE to The Committee for the Page-Barbour and James W. Richard Lectures, and in particular to their chairman, Dr. Walker Cowen, Director of the University Press of Virginia, for the invitation they extended to me to deliver the James. W. Richard Lectures at the University of Virginia, Charlottesville. It is a great honor and a joy to be associated in this way with such a lovely and distinguished university. My warm thanks are offered to the departments of religious studies and of physics, who received and entertained me so generously and gave me every encouragement and support. I am especially indebted to Professor David B. Harned, head of the department of religious studies, who ever since he studied with me many years ago in Edinburgh has been a very good friend and whose signal achievements in administration, teaching, and beautiful theological writing I have admired from afar.

At the same time I would like to take this opportunity to say how much I appreciate the regular hospitality extended to me by President James I. McCord and Princeton Theological Seminary in my visits to the United States. Four of the lectures included here were given in an earlier form at the seminary's Summer Institute in July 1977.

Acknowledgment is gratefully made to The Templeton Foundation, Nassau, and the Lismore Press, Dublin, for permission to incorporate in Chapter one, the address given at the sixth presentation of the Templeton Foundation Prize for Progress in Religion at Guildhall, London, on Tuesday, 11 March 1978.

Once more I have been greatly helped by my younger son, the Rev. Iain R. Torrance, who has taken time out of his own scholarly work to help me with the proofs and to prepare the index. It is a joy to be grateful to him.

My indebtedness to my wife, Margaret, is unbounded. Few theologians can have been so blessed by the unflagging love and patience and support that she has given me, not least when my thoughts have been locked up in long hours and days of concentration. *Laus Deo.*

I

Man

the Priest of Creation

THE ULTIMATE END of Christian theology is undoubtedly the knowledge and enjoyment of God for his own sake, but this knowledge and enjoyment arise within the relation of God the Creator to the universe he has made and within which he has set man, who is known within traditional theology as "the crown of creation." It is in and through the universe of space and time that God has revealed himself to us in modes of rationality that he has conferred upon the creation and upon us in the creation, and it is in and through the same universe of space and time that theology makes its disciplined response to God's self-revelation. The understanding of this universe, which is the prime aim of our natural scientific inquiries, can only be of deep interest to theology. This is God's universe, which he made accessible to our inquiries, and it is precisely in this universe that we worship and enjoy him and seek to fulfill the divinely given purpose for intelligent human beings in its creation. That is why I make no apology as a theologian for my own engagement over the years in trying to think out the interrelations of theological and natural science, for, as I understand it, this is part of my calling as man of faith and man of science.

At no time, perhaps, has this theological interest in natural science been so intense as it is now, in view of the startling advances recently made in a unitary and comprehensive understanding of the whole space-time manifold. Before the astonishing nature of the universe as it is revealed in scientific inquiry, I am overwhelmed with awe and wonder of a profoundly religious kind, in which my prime thought is of praise and glory to God the Father Almighty, Maker of heaven and earth and of all things visible and invisible.

> When I look at the sky, which you have made,
> at the moon and the stars, which you
> set in their places—
> what is man, that you think of him;
> mere man, that you care for him?   (Psalm 8:3–4)

How often those words from the ancient psalm of Israel have echoed in our thoughts as the incomprehensible immensity of the universe began to be disclosed to the inquiries of our astronomers! Vast as our solar system is, the sun is only one star among the one hundred-thousand million stars that make up our own galaxy, which we call the Milky Way. The Milky Way is so immense that light traveling at the rate of approximately 186,000 miles a second would take 100,000 years to pass from one end of it to the other. But the Milky Way is only one galaxy among at least

100,000,000 similar systems of stars far beyond it. And what is also staggering is that this universe, comprising all these galaxies, is expanding at the rate of more than 160,000 miles a second. What is man, mere man, in the face of this incomprehensible immensity, that God should think of him and care for him?

And now, as if in answer to that question, our astronomers have come up with something that to me is even more breath-taking in its implications: the narrow margin of possibility that all this allows for the rise of intelligent life anywhere in the universe. I refer here to the F. W. Angel Memorial Lecture delivered by Sir Bernard Lovell in Newfoundland in October 1977 (now incorporated in his book *In the Center of Immensities*), in which he asked: Why is the universe expanding so near the critical rate to prevent its collapse? If the universe had begun to expand in the first few minutes after the explosion of its original incredibly dense state by a rate minutely slower than it did, it would have collapsed back again relatively quickly. And if the expansion of the universe had been different only by a tiny fraction one way or the other from its actual rate, human existence would evidently have been impossible. "But our *measurements*," Sir Bernard declared, "narrowly define one such universe—which had to be that particular universe if it was ever to be known and comprehended by an intelligent being" (p. 116).

All this seems to say two things. First, this vast universe is the kind of universe it is because it is necessary for the existence of man: somehow man and the universe are profoundly bracketed together. Many years ago when Einstein first formulated the theory of general relativity, Hermann Weyl pointed out that since all things, bodies in motion and space and time, are ultimately defined by reference to light, light occupies a unique metaphysical place in the universe. Now, however, even from the way that astrophysical science is developing, it appears that man occupies a unique metaphysical place in the universe. It is in this direction that science was pointed by Professor John Archibald Wheeler, then of Princeton, in a lecture given in 1973 in commemoration of the 500th anniversary of the birth of Copernicus, which he entitled "The Universe as Home for Man." And it is much the same theme that Sir John Eccles has taken up recently in his Gifford Lectures in Edinburgh.

Second, the fact that the universe has expanded in such a way that the emergence of conscious mind in it is an essential property of the universe, must surely mean that we cannot give an adequate account of the universe in its astonishing structure and harmony without taking conscious mind into account, that is, without including conscious mind as an essential factor in our scientific equations. That is a point that Shrödinger made as long ago as 1958 in his Cambridge lectures published under the title *Mind and Matter*, and that Sir John Eccles took up in his work *Facing Reality* in 1970. If this is the case, as I believe it is, then natural science is on the verge of opening itself out toward higher levels of reality in a movement of wonder and awe in which our increasing awareness of the limitations of science—the theme of Sir Bernard Lovell's presidential lecture to the British Association for the Advance of Science in 1974—is matched by our awareness that as we probe into the intrinsic order of the universe, we are in touch with a depth of intelligibility that reaches indefinitely beyond what our finite minds can comprehend. I cannot but recall here those sentences of Einstein's in which he spoke of "that humble attitude of mind towards the grandeur of reason incarnate in existence, and which, in its profoundest depths is inaccessible to man" (*Out of My Later Years*, p. 33), and of "the rapturous amazement at the harmony of natural law, which reveals an intelligence of such superiority that, compared with it, all systematic thinking and acting of human beings is an utterly insignificant reflection" (*The World as I See It*, p. 18).

To all this, theological science presents a complementary account, for this universe of space and time explored by natural science—far from being alien—is the universe in which God has planted us. He created the universe and endowed man with gifts of mind and understanding to investigate and interpret it. Just as he made life to reproduce itself, so he has made the universe—with man as an essential constituent of it—in such a way that it can bring forth and articulate knowledge of itself. Our scientific knowledge of the universe as it unfolds its secrets to our human inquiries is itself part of the expanding universe. Regarded in this light the pursuit of natural science is one of the ways in which man, the child of God, fulfills his distinctive function in the creation. That is how, for example, Francis Bacon at the outset of our modern scientific era understood the work of human science as a form of man's obedience to God. Science properly pursued in this way is a religious duty. Man as scientist can be spoken of as the priest of creation, whose office it is to interpret the books of nature written by the finger of God, to unravel the universe in its marvelous patterns and symmetries, and to bring it all into orderly articulation in such a way that it fulfills its proper end as the vast theater of glory in which the Creator is wor-

[5

shipped and hymned and praised by his creatures. Without man, nature is dumb, but it is man's part to give it word: to be its mouth through which the whole universe gives voice to the glory and majesty of the living God.

This is the universe of space and time through which God has also revealed himself personally to man in historical dialogue with the human race, which has involved the establishment of communities of reciprocity in which his Word is intelligibly mediated to us and knowledge of God becomes communicable through Holy Scriptures. But since all this takes place within the created universe of space and time, and since space and time are the bearers of all rational order within the universe, it is in and through this universe as its orderly connections are unfolded under man's scientific investigations that we are surely to develop and express our knowledge of God mediated through his Word. The natural scientist and the theologian are both at work within the same space-time structures of the universe and under the limits of their boundary conditions. The natural scientist inquires into the processes and patterns of nature, and man himself is a part of nature; and the theologian inquires of God the Creator of nature and the source of its created rationalities, to which man also belongs. Thus theological science and natural science have their own proper and distinctive objectives to pursue, but their work inevitably overlaps, for they both respect and operate through the same rational structures of space and time, while each develops special modes of investigation, rationality, and verification in accordance with the nature and the direction of its distinctive field. But since each of them is the kind of thing it is as a human inquiry because of the profound correlation between human knowing and the space-time structures of the creation, each is in its depth akin to the other.

Regarded in this way, natural science and theological science are not opponents but partners before God, in a service of God in which each may learn from the other how better to pursue its own distinctive function, how better to be natural science or how better to be theological science. This is a relationship that is not one-sided but mutual, for natural science has actually learned far more from theological science than is generally realized. In a lecture I gave in July of 1978 in New York to the International Institute of Theoretic Sciences (to which I shall refer extensively in the third chapter), I showed how three of the most basic ideas of modern natural science—which have come very much to the front since general relativity—go back to definite roots, and indeed derive from Christian sources, in Alexandria, as Greek theologians from the fourth to the sixth century thought out the relation between the Incarnation and the Creation and reconstructed the foundations of ancient science and culture. But let me give you now a different example, taken from James Clerk Maxwell, whose death a hundred years ago we commemorated in 1979. The distinctive idea he used in developing his celebrated field theory—which has had such a powerful impact on modern science, not least upon the thought of Einstein—Clerk Maxwell gained as a student in Edinburgh University, not so much from his classes in physics as from Sir William Hamilton's lectures in metaphysics, an idea that had a theological as well as a philosophical root. It is cross-fertilization of this kind that is to be found behind some of the most outstanding advances in human knowledge. But the great day for creative integration between apparently separate or opposing disciplines, such as natural science and theological science, lies, not behind us, but ahead of us. This kind of dialogue and exchange in thought is now possible in a new and exciting way because of far-reaching change that has been going on within the foundations of knowledge, in which both science and theology have been sharing in different ways.

Since it is this deepening coordination in understanding between natural science and theological science that I have tried to serve, it may be of interest if I indicate briefly how I regard this change in scientific activity that makes such coordination possible.

The fundamental principle that I have been concerned with is a very simple one, but its implications are deep and far-reaching when worked out consistently over the whole range of human knowledge. We know things in accordance with their natures, or what they are in themselves; and so we let the nature of what we know determine for us the content and form of our knowledge. This is what happens in our ordinary, everyday experience and knowledge, when, for example, we treat trees in accordance with their nature as trees and not as rocks, or treat cows in accordance with their nature as cows and not as horses, or treat human beings in accordance with their nature as persons and not as things. Science, in every field of our human experience, is only the rigorous extension of that basic way of thinking and behaving. This is a way of understanding scientific activity that is much more appropriate to the complexity and richness of nature as it becomes disclosed to us through the great advances of the special sciences than is that way to which we became accustomed within the compass of a mechanistic universe and its rigid instrumentalism. This is particularly evident in the field of biology, where advance has been obstructed through reduction of organismic relations into mechanistic concepts. Nature must be respected and courted, not imposed upon. We must let it develop and flower, as it were, under our investigations. That is surely required if we are really to know anything in accordance with what it is in itself, and not simply along the lines of its artificial reaction to our tormenting distortion of it. Science is not, therefore, something to be set against our ordinary and natural experience in the world, but, on the contrary, is a development and a refinement of it, with a deeper penetration into the natural coherences and patterns already embedded in the real world and already governing our normal behavior day by day.

All this applies as much in our relations with God as in our relations with nature or with one another. There is no secret way of knowing either in science or in theology, but there is only one basic way of knowing, which naturally develops different modes of rationality in natural science and in theological science because the nature of what we seek to know in each is different—and that is a difference we are rationally and scientifically obliged to respect. Thus it would be unscientific to transfer from one field to another the distinctive mode of rationality that develops within it. Just as it would be irrational to try to know a person by subjecting his physical existence to chemical analysis or to treat a chemical substance as though it were a human being and to try to talk to it and listen to it, so it would be irrational to look for God through a telescope or to treat him like a natural process—as irrational as it would be to use God as a stopgap in the formation of some hypothesis to explain a set of physical connections in nature.

In each field of inquiry, then, we must be faithful to the reality we seek to know and must act and think always in a relation of relentless fidelity to that reality. This is why we cannot oppose natural science and theological science to each other as though they could or had to contradict one another, but must, rather, regard them as applying the one basic way of knowing faithfully to their respective fields and must seek to coordinate the knowledge they yield through the appropriate modes of inquiry and thought they develop.

In recent years the increasing fidelity of science to the nature of things has resulted in a number of changes that are proving to be highly significant for the unification of knowledge in overcoming the split between the natural and the human sciences and between both of these and theological science. Let me refer to four of these changes.

1. Science has been shedding its abstractive character, in which, through a predominantly observationalist approach, it tended to tear the surface patterns of things away from their objective ground in reality, as though we could have no knowledge of things in themselves or in their internal relations, but only in their appearances to us. That abstractive method involved the damaging bifurcation in nature with which the deep splits in our modern culture are associated. But now all that is being cut back, as—in sheer faithfulness to things as they actually are in themselves—science is concerned to understand the surface patterns of things in the light of the natural coherences in which they are actually embedded, and it therefore operates with the indissoluble unity of form and being, or of theoretical and empirical elements

in human knowledge. Here we have a reconciling force in the depths of scientific knowledge that cannot help but heal the breaches that have opened in our culture. Not only can theological science share in this reconciliation, it can make a creative contribution to it.

2. The great era of merely analytical science is now coming to an end, for the new science (if I can call it that) starting from a unitary approach, operates with an integration of form that transcends the limits of analytical methods and their disintegrating effects. Atomistic thinking is replaced by relational thinking—nowhere is that more true than in the development of high-energy physics and particle theory, in which many of the so-called particles are recognized, not as discrete particles, but as energy knots in the fields of force between the stronger particles. Here we have a mode of onto-relational thinking with which Christian theology has long been familiar—out of which, for example, there came the concept of the person. But let us look at the change in another way. Merely analytical science has had great difficulty in coping with the problem of how to think together being and event or the geometrical and the dynamic aspects of nature, such as the particle and the field in light theory, or position and momentum in quantum theory. Although Einstein failed to develop a unified field theory that would transcend the divergent corpuscular and undulatory theories of light, he insisted that any real description of nature in its internal relations must involve the unity of the particle and the field, as indeed Faraday had already indicated in the last century. As I understand it, this is the stage that high-energy physics has now reached. But in Christian

theology this stage had already been reached by Karl Barth forty years ago, when with herculean effort he brought together the ancient emphasis upon the being of God in his acts and the modern emphasis upon the acts of God in his being, and thus integrated in a remarkable way the whole history of Christian thought. It is integrative thinking of this kind, whether in natural or in theological science, that is bound to have the greatest effect in the future upon all our human knowledge.

3. One of the most startling features in recent science is the success with which scientists like Katsir and Prigogine have wrestled with the problem of how to relate the so-called random elements in nature to the laws of thermodynamics, which—as classically formulated—hold only within closed systems. Katsir tragically lost his life in the Lod airport massacre a few years ago, but Prigogine has recently been given the Nobel Prize for work in which he has applied the laws of thermodynamics to open, or non-equilibrium, systems. It is difficult to grasp all that this means, but what does seem clear to me is that the old way of thinking in terms of the couplets chance and necessity, uncertainty and determinism, must now be replaced by a new way of thinking in terms of spontaneity and open-structured order—for what is revealed to us is an astonishing spontaneity in nature that yields a dynamic kind of order with an indefinite range of intelligibility that cries out for completion beyond the universe known to our natural scientific inquiries. Theologically speaking, what we are concerned with here is an understanding of the spontaneity and freedom of the created universe as grounded in the unlimited spontaneity and

freedom of God the Creator. Here natural science and theological science bear closely upon one another at their boundary conditions, and what is needed is a more adequate doctrine of creation, in which knowledge from both sides of those boundary conditions can be coordinated.

4. Science has been moving away from a flat understanding of nature all on one level to one that is characterized by a hierarchy of levels, or dimensions. Science of this kind is concerned to discover the relations between things and events at different levels of complexity. It has the double task of penetrating into a new kind of connection and of lifting up the mind to a new level where we can apprehend and bring that new kind of connection to appropriate formulation. The universe is not flat, but is a stratified structure, so that our science takes the form of an ascending hierarchy of relations of thought that are open upward in a deeper and deeper dimension of depth but that cannot be flattened downward by being reduced to connections all on the same level. The old-fashioned science that tried to reduce everything to hard, causal connections in a rigidly mechanistic universe damaged the advance of knowledge in all the higher levels with which we are concerned in our culture. But advance of this kind is now going on, for the new science gives ample room for the human sciences and the sciences of the spirit, and for all sciences concerned with living connections, within the framework of an open-structured dynamic universe in which the human person is not suffocated, but can breathe freely transcendent air, and yet be profoundly concerned with scientific understanding of

the whole complex of connections that make up our universe. No one has pioneered this way of heuristic thinking in science more than Michael Polanyi, whose thought reveals an unrivaled subtlety and delicacy in showing how the different levels of human understanding are coordinated in such a semantic focus that meaning is brought back to our world with new force and direction. Here, instead of fragmenting in disintegrating specializations, the whole enterprise of science recovers in depth and breadth an uplifting unitary outlook that begins to match the character of the universe itself—and indeed the relation of the universe to God its transcendent Creator and Sustainer.

It is more and more clear to me that, under the providence of God, owing to these changes in the very foundations of knowledge in which natural and theological science alike have been sharing, the damaging cultural splits between the sciences and the humanities and between both of these and theology, are in process of being overcome, that the destructive and divisive forces too long rampant in world-wide human life and thought are being undermined, and that a massive new synthesis will emerge in which man, humbled and awed by the mysterious intelligibility of the universe that reaches far beyond his powers, will learn to fulfill his destined role as the servant of divine love and the priest of creation.

2

Emerging from the Cultural Split

THE PURPOSE OF THIS LECTURE is to take a hard look at contemporary theology from the perspective of dogmatics and science, within the scientific transition from a *dualist* to a *unitary* outlook upon the universe. This is a transition that profoundly affects our understanding of dogmatics and of science, and of their intimate connection with one another, which I shall try to make clear as the lectures proceed. But let me explain briefly at the outset what I mean by *dogmatics* and by *science*. By *dogmatics* I mean the pure science of theology: not some system of ideas laid down on the ground of external preconceptions and authorities, nor some useless, abstract stuff concerned with detached, merely academic questions, nor again some man-centered ideology that we think up for ourselves out of our socio-political involvements with one another, but the actual knowledge of the living God as he is disclosed to us through his interaction with us in our world of space and time—knowledge of God that is ultimately controlled by the nature of God as he is in himself. By *science* I mean, for the most part, natural science in its pure rather than in its applied forms: that is, not something worked up in accordance with *a priori* assumptions and imposed as law upon nature nor merely convenient arrangements of observational data that we can put to practical use in our human attempts to triumph over nature, but rather the knowledge we reach of things in any field under the compulsion of their independent reality, in controlled reference to their inherent nature, and formulated in the light of their internal relations.

Many of our contemporaries, of course, are frightened to relate theology and science and operate with a practical segregation between them, relegating to each its own autonomous sphere of intelligibility and justification. Tragic as this is when, for example, it leads people to cut off faith in Christ from the historical Jesus, it says a great deal about our contemporary scene. It shows that modern theology of this kind has isolated itself from the all-important relation between God and the world of space and time, confining itself to severely truncated man-God relations, and it has thereby lost any common basis in the intelligibility of the created universe. This is evidently what lies behind the inability of so many contemporary theologians to enter into serious dialogue with natural science, for they have no common ground upon which to establish connections with it.

On the other hand, something very different is found happening among men of science, who more and more number themselves among believers. Indeed, among scientists in not a few universities known to me, there is a higher proportion of believers than outside the universities. This is an indication of a profound transition in outlook relating to the advance of science itself that theologians have not adequately appreciated. Basic habits of knowing are being changed as we are liberated from the restrictive and abstractive modes of thought that have prevailed for so long in our Western culture. Different dimensions of reality, once foreclosed, are now more accessible, indicating a multi-leveled universe that requires on our part the development of conceptions and structures of thought that are both more open and more deeply and naturally grounded in the astonishing intelligibility of the universe. Here the scientist can no longer confine his thought within the brackets of his artificially imposed abstractions, but must find ways of lifting it again and again to new levels of connection, for the intelligibility of the universe that he seeks to grasp in its ontological depth will not be reduced to any one level, but penetrates through them all. Moreover, since this very intelligibility with which he has to do in natural science transcends the limits of his natural-scientific methods, the scientist, if he is to remain faithful to that intelligibility and thus remain rational, must commit himself to it and must open his mind to it beyond the point of its accessibility to natural science. Hence, scientists today frequently find themselves at the frontiers and limits of their science compelled to ask open questions directed toward an intelligible ground beyond the determinations of science, but without which science would not ultimately be consistent or make sense. In other words, the more scientific inquiry presses toward the boundary conditions of intelligibility in the physical universe—whether in its microscopic or in its macroscopic aspects—the more scientists find themselves thrust up against the question of the creation and the Creator. It is understandable, therefore, that not a few scientists today should be concerned to establish connections with theology and, what is more, are found demanding a proper theology of creation that by and large they do not get. Precisely at the point where the world of natural science needs dialogue with theology, it is badly let down, for modern theology, as I have said, has so deprived itself of a common basis in the intelligibility of the created universe that it is unable to share in the astonishing advance of scientific knowledge and even feels its isolation and cherished autonomy threatened by the scientific transition toward a unitary outlook upon the universe.

Undoubtedly the immediate fears of these theologians, and their cultivated separation of theology from science, are tied up with false notions of science as well as of theology. Particularly damaging in its influence upon them, however, has been the prevalent conception, obsolete though it is, of the universe as a mechanistic system, or a closed continuum of cause and effect, characterized throughout by a hard determinism. As an instance of this some of you may recall Rudolf Bultmann's view of the world in which even history figures as a closed continuum of effects regarded as individual events connected by the succession of cause and effect. With this initial assumption, he had to rule out of court anything like incarnation or miracle or resurrection, on the ground that they would rupture the continuum of historical happenings through the alleged interference of supernatural, transcendent powers. But he had also to rule out of consideration any objective act of God within the cosmos, for example, in the crucifixion of

Christ, which in point of fact emptied the atonement of any real saving content for men and women of flesh and blood within this world of space and time. The effect of all this was to make Bultmann offer an existentialist reinterpretation of the Christian message, in which it would be made safe from the critical investigation of science—or, otherwise expressed, in which the advances of scientific understanding of the universe would be quite irrelevant for Christian existence and faith. Such a segregation of Christianity from science, of course, also has the effect of making it impossible for Christian theology or ethics to have any impact on the development or deployment of modern science and technology.

Behind all this lies a disastrous dualism to which we shall return shortly. First, however, I would like to point up the contrast between this attitude toward science on the part of Bultmann and others and the position actually adopted by scientists themselves, by referring to an illuminating meeting of two international academies of science and theology, held recently on Long Island, at which the theme for discussion, chosen by the scientists, was "determinism and free creation." All the scientists reading papers showed by arguments in mathematics, physics, thermodynamics, and the philosophy of science that the era of determinism had come to an end. In contrast, however, we had one Continental theologian who spoke of "the iron determinisms of nature" as though he had not listened to any of the lectures given and was quite unaware of the profound changes going on in the foundations of scientific knowledge; another Continental theologian so spiritualized away the resurrection and the new creation in a contrast between theology and science that one of the eminent physicists present came up to me afterwards to say that he wanted some reality in theology, a proper understanding of creation and resurrection. There the discrepancy between scientists and theologians could hardly have been greater, at least as far as those two theologians were concerned. This is a discrepancy, however, that manifests itself not only in the relations of theology and science but in the widespread malaise of the split culture that came to its sharpest peak in the 1960s, but from which we are now steadily emerging.

The problem that now faces us in contemporary theology is this: while scientists have moved on, far beyond the narrow mechanistic determinisms of the Laplacians or the Marxists, to a profounder and more unitary grasp of the intelligible connections in the contingent order of the universe, theology tends, for the most part, to remain stuck in obscurantist modes of thought that have their roots in the radical dualisms of the past. And the so-called liberal theology that plies its free-thinking within the carefully guarded autonomous status of man's religious and moral experience easily slips into empty humanist subjectivism, even when eked out by some kind of mystical transcendentalism—it is evidently the least able to establish intelligible connections with natural science and to share in a common advance to a deeper and more unitary understanding of the universe of space and time as the orderly creation of the one Triune God.

On the other hand, fundamental changes have been taking place in present-day theology, with developments of a positive and integrative nature that share in the transition from a dualist to a unitary outlook in the universe, so that the future holds for scientists and theologians alike a more adequate grasp of creation and incarnation and of their implications for creative reconstruction in the foundations of human culture. I hope to say something about this in subsequent lectures, but meantime I want to concentrate on the problem of dualism and its effects in our theology, for it is as well to understand as fully as we can in this transitional period the state of affairs from which we are emerging if we are to take full advantage of the possibilities for constructive developments in scientific theology in the years ahead.

The form of dualism with which we are concerned took its definitive shape through the thought of Kant and Descartes or of Newton and Galileo, but it goes back through the Christian centuries to the foundations of classical Western culture in Greece. I refer here to the irreducible dualisms in the philosophy and cosmology of Plato and Aristotle, which threw into sharp contrast rectilinear motion in terrestrial mechanics and circular motion in celestial mechanics, which were related to the dualisms between the empirical and the theoretical, the physical and the spiritual, the temporal and the eternal, the mortal and the divine. Attempts were made, notably by the atomists, to reduce this radical bifurcation through a unitary theory of motion, apparently at the expense of higher, spiritual dimensions of reality. They never succeeded, but instead these dualisms congealed, as it were, through the Aristotelian notion of *chorismos*, or separation, into the comprehensive dualism of the Ptolemaic cosmology between the supralunar and infralunar realms, which inevitably affected all life and thought within its framework right up to the scientific revolution associated with Copernicus and Galileo.

Developments of the greatest significance came through

Greek Christian theology, of which I shall speak in the following lecture, but by and large the dualist outlook of later, Neoplatonic Hellenism came to prevail and was given its most enduring and masterful expression in the Augustinian culture of Western Christendom. Here God and the world, heaven and earth, the eternal and the temporal, were so sharply separated that great attempts were made to clamp them together; and so with the help of resurrected Aristotelian philosophy and science, a great synthesis emerged in which theology and science were intimately connected with one another in a unified, rational outlook upon God and the world. Yet the price paid for this synthesis was considerable, for the causal and logical bridge thrown across the chasm between God and the world was possible only through introducing Aristotelian ideas of God, man, nature, motion, and causality into the heart of medieval theology, deeply affecting the Christian doctrines of God and the soul and the mediation between God and man. Far from overcoming the Augustinian dualism in the heart of medieval Christendom, this development narrowed and hardened it and tied theology to obsolete notions of science, metaphysics, and psychology, but it did succeed in connecting theological and scientific concepts in such a way that theology and science shared together in the developing understanding of a rationally ordered universe so essential for the rise of modern science.

However, when the Aristotelian network of science, metaphysics, and psychology that underpinned the medieval synthesis succumbed to the critical attacks of Reformation theology and Galilean science, the old radical dualism reappeared and was considerably reinforced through Renaissance Neoplatonism and Reformation Augustinianism, as also indeed through Galileo's far-reaching distinction between primary and secondary qualities, or between geometry and appearance. Hence, even while the Ptolemaic cosmological outlook gave way before the Copernican revolution, the new era ushered in with Galileo continued to be characterized by an inveterate dualism that was given its philosophical expression by Descartes and Locke and its scientific expression by Isaac Newton—who built into his great system of the world the massive dualism between absolute mathematical time and space and relative apparent time and space that was to become paradigmatic for all modern science and cosmology up to Einstein. This development gave rise to the deistic disjunction between God and the universe that has so deeply plagued modern theology and to the conception of the mechanistic universe, which closed the universe to any interaction with it on the part of the Creator. Moreover, because with Newton time as well as space became part of the essential subject-matter of science, other human sciences such as history became caught up into the Newtonian dualism. This is very evident, for example, in the ugly big ditch that Lessing claimed to find between necessary truths of reason and accidental truths of history, but where more evident than in Herrmann's distinction between two kinds of history, *Historie* and *Geschichte*, which has so bedeviled modern biblical interpretation?

Now the particular form of this dualism most damaging to theology is that which derives from the thought of Immanuel Kant. Let me indicate briefly how that came about. Newton took over the Galilean distinction between the geometric aspects of reality, which are quantifiable, and those aspects called appearances or phenomena, which are not quantifiable as such, but which must nevertheless be correlated with what is quantifiable if we are to make scientific or mechanical sense of our observable world. In order to cope with this, Newton deployed his distinction between absolute mathematical time and space and relative apparent time and space. Through clamping down the former, regarded as an unchangeable, inertial framework, upon the world of observations and appearances, characterized by relative apparent time and space, he was able to bring mathematical order into phenomena, and so to expound the immutable laws of nature in terms of the causal and mechanical connections that constitute the system of the world. Newton himself identified absolute time and space with the mind and presence of God—he called it the divine "sensorium"—for it is, he held, the mind and presence of the eternal, immutable God, as an inertial frame, that contains the universe, holding it together in such a way as to impart to it rational order, consistency, and stability. This was important for Newton, for it meant that the rational order of the universe with which we are concerned in scientific formulation is objectively grounded in the created universe, irrespective of the human observer. Thus the human knower is in touch with rational structures that are true independently of his observations and indeed are not affected by them, yet these structures are clamped together with the phenomenal universe through the containing power of God, in what might be called a grand mythological synthesis of God and the universe.

The Galilean dualism between the geometrical and observational aspects of reality took another form in the thought of Descartes, who operated with the notion of innate ideas in the human mind and intuitively-comprehended axioms, on the one hand, and a materialist, mechanistic view of nature and extension, or space, on the other hand—but he regarded these as held together by God the Creator of the mental and material realms as the common cause of motion. While the emphasis here fell upon the geometrical aspects of reality, and thus upon rationalism and deductivism, it was otherwise with Locke, who returned to the old Aristotelian idea that there is nothing in the mind except what first comes through the senses, and thus developed a dualism between mental substances and material substances in which the stress fell upon the latter. He rejected the notion of innate ideas and held that ideas arose in the mind only through impressions made upon it by external or material substances—that is to say, he held that the only ideas the mind can have are derived from sense experience or from reflections upon sense data. This sensationism, as Hume saw so clearly, plays havoc with the connection between cause and effect that was so all-important for Newtonian science, for it emptied causality of any objective character. If all we have in basic knowledge is reduced to streams of impressions or associations of sense data, then it is impossible to deduce that, within any sequence of phenomena, one phenomenon is cause and another effect.

Hume's analysis forced upon Kant the necessity of finding some way of bringing the empirical and the theoretical ingredients in knowledge together if the foundations of Newtonian science were to be saved. This he did through his theory of "the synthetic *a priori*," in which he combined sense experience, not with innate ideas, but with built-in structures of the consciousness through which the human knower imposed conceptual order on all he perceived, so that it was impossible for him ever to penetrate behind his cognitive activity to what things are in themselves, independent of his perceiving and conceiving. With reference, then, to Newton's dualism, what Kant did was to transfer absolute time and space from the mind of God to the mind of the human knower, where they retain their "absolute" character, i.e., are not affected or modified by experience—which meant that instead of reading laws of nature out of nature, man ultimately reads them into nature through the processes and structures of his active reason. Moreover, when Kant gave to time and space the status of "forms of sensibility," and to causality as well as to substance the status of "categories of the understanding," he rejected the possibility of any knowledge of things in themselves, limiting knowledge of them to what we can make out of their appearances. Further, he introduced such an element of necessity into the very act of knowing that he generalized the determinism of Newtonian physics for all human science and all human knowledge, thus making determinism into a hard metaphysical dogma.

All this involved a very damaging dualism that not only cut deeply into human knowledge but cut sharply across it. It demanded a bifurcation between unknowable "things in themselves," to be treated as no more than hypothetical entities, and what is scientifically knowable, namely, completely determined and necessary objects; or more generally, a bifurcation between a realm of noumenal essences and ideas from a realm of phenomenal objects and events. This implied a deep split in human experience: between the experience of man as a being in the world of phenomena, where he has no freedom, and the experience of man as a subject of the supersensual, or noumenal, world, where his only freedom belongs—which, not unnaturally, had the effect of giving rise to a romantic idealism where the human spirit could range at will, uncontrolled by scientific evidence or knowledge. But by limiting scientific knowledge to what is observable and phenomenally determinate, Kant severed the connection between science and faith, depriving faith of any objective or ontological reference and emptying it of any real cognitive content. That is the difficult context of thought in which Schleiermacher and Ritschl and their followers struggled to find some worthy place in human culture for the Christian message; but the whole history of nineteenth- and twentieth-century theology demonstrates that so long as people operate with an axiomatic disjunction between a noumenal realm of ideas and a phenomenal realm of events, nothing more than a merely moral or poetic or symbolic or mythological meaning can be given to the biblical account of the saving interaction of God with us in the world of space and time, or to the Christian message of the incarnation, crucifixion, and resurrection of Jesus Christ. It is the anachronistic persistence of the conception of the world as a closed, deterministic realm of causal connections that keeps alive the damaging dualisms that give rise to such pseudo-interpretations and pseudo-theologies, which are still so rife; but as those dualisms collapse in a scientific transition to a unitary outlook upon the universe, which is what is now taking place, the apparent justification for these pseudo-interpretations and pseudo-theologies collapses as well—and that too is now taking place.

I do not wish to probe further into the historical roots

of dualism, but would like instead to go on to show something of the effect of dualist modes of thought upon theology.

1. *The effect of dualism upon biblical interpretation*

In line with what we have just been discussing, let me refer to the positivist restriction of knowledge to observational phenomena. According to this view, we derive the rational components of knowledge, such as scientific theories, by deducing them from our observations—for there is, it is alleged, no direct cognitive access to rational forms or theoretical structures, but only indirect access by way of logical inference. The effect of this upon biblical interpretation is two-fold.

(*a*) By cutting out any possibility of immediate apprehension of rational or intelligible elements in any field of investigation, dualism limits the theological component in biblical knowledge to what is logically derived from observations or appearances. Behind this, of course, there lies the Kantian idea that we cannot know things in themselves or in their internal relations, but only in their external relations as they appear to us, so that things can be incorporated as "objects" into our knowledge only as we bring extrinsic theoretical factors to bear upon them from the structures of our consciousness. This means, for example, that it is impossible for us ever to know anything of Jesus Christ as he is in himself, for we are restricted to Jesus as he appeared to his contemporaries—and indeed to the impression he made upon them as it is mediated through the structures of their consciousness, by which they made him an "object" of their faith and knowledge. It will thus be the task of the biblical scholar, through some form of "the historico-critical method," to bring to view and to clarify as far as he can the impression Jesus made as he actually appeared to his contemporaries, stripped of any theological interpretation put upon him in the course of the developing tradition—for by definition such theological elements cannot have intrinsic rootage in Jesus himself. This means that only after the biblical scholar has established by some set of criteria what are acceptable as observational data, shorn clean of any theoretical components, may the theologian go to work on them to deduce from them valid theological ideas or doctrines. This of course yields a rather nominalist notion of theology similar to the nominalist and conventionalist conception of scientific theory or natural law held by the positivists, e.g., Ernst Mach.

(b) The restriction of knowledge to what is observable or to what may be deduced from observations, operates only with the epistemological model of vision, thereby casting its dualism into the form of a visible realm, to which we have access only by intuition, and an invisible realm, to which we have access only by logical inference or hypothetico-deductive activity. The denial of any direct cognitive access to intelligible reality entailed here—which, as we saw earlier, empties faith of cognitive content—is considerably reinforced by the limitation of intuitive apprehension to visual or aesthetic experience, for it cuts out the possibility of intuitive acts in auditive experience and ignores the deep interconnection between understanding and word and between faith and hearing. The effect of this is to undermine the all-important place of *word* in the Scriptures, which not only empties the biblical material of its distinctive rational form but thereby also undermines the necessity for a thoroughly theological interpretation of the Scriptures. The dualism at work behind this approach cuts off the word of the Scriptures from the objective Word of God, which is the immediately apprehended theoretical ingredient in God's self-revelation to man and in man's knowledge of God—for by definition, in the deistic disjunction between God and the world demanded by this dualism, there can be no interaction between God and our world of space and time. The effect of all this is to transpose the biblical material into a very different genre: of picture and image, symbol and myth, where at best we may have only some tangential or indirect relation to God and correspondingly only "oblique truth" about him—which critical minds have little difficulty in showing to be empty and meaningless.

This whole approach to biblical interpretation reposes upon the epistemological dualism between the empirical and the theoretical devastatingly destroyed by Einstein when he established, as in general relativity, the indissoluble unity of form and being, or the theoretical and empirical factors in knowledge, in such a way as to show that our basic scientific concepts are reached, not by logical deduction or inference from observations, but through immediate intuition or apprehension of an intellective kind. We appre-

hend intelligible structures inherent in the universe immediately, although doubtless for the most part along with
sensible or phenomenal objects and events. This "extra-
logical" apprehension of unobservable intelligible structures is not to be confounded, however, with their formal
justification or methodological establishment in the body
of our knowledge, which may require axiomatic and hypothetico-deductive procedures.

Now the intelligibility inherent in the universe that
Einstein was concerned to grasp and articulate in physics
and cosmology is, of course of the kind that is amenable to
mathematical representation—that is, intelligibility that
takes the rational form of "number." But the intelligibility
with which we are concerned in biblical interpretation and
theology is the kind that takes the rational form of *logos*, or
"word." That is why the basic statements with which we
have to do in theology are what I have called elsewhere
"hearing statements," or "heard statements," which corre-
spond closely to the "recognition statements," or the basic
statements, with which we have to do in mathematics or
physics. These are statements of the kind that we are forced
to make as our minds fall under the power of the intrinsic
rationality of the field we are investigating; not statements
that we think up for ourselves, but statements imposed
upon us by objective structural relations, which we express
aright when we are faithful to the ontological integrity of
the unity of form and being, structure and substance, that
reality discloses of itself. Thus, *mutatis mutandis*, what
holds good of our apprehension of objective intelligibility
in nature, holds good also of our apprehension of objective
intelligibility in the biblical revelation, which we call the
Word of God.

Thus, with the exposure and collapse of the false epistemological dualism with which so much modern biblical interpretation is bound up, the ground is clear for us to engage in a fresh theological interpretation of the biblical material, through which it will be presented to us in a very different light. Theological structures may be developed only if they are directly grounded in, and epistemically controlled by, the objective intelligibilities of the biblical revelation, such as the intrinsic significance of Jesus, the Word made flesh.

2 *The effect of dualism upon theological statements*

Here let us look at things from a slightly different angle, and think of dualism as that which arises when we abstract the phenomenal surface of our experience, or the world of appearances, from the geometrical frame on which it is grounded. When that happens, the phenomenal surface inevitably starts to disintegrate, for it loses contact with the objective structures that hold the appearances together in coherent and meaningful patterns. This is evident in the whole history of thought, but perhaps nowhere more evident today than in the developing disintegration of form in art—which can be traced back to the impressionists in their desire to separate the sensuous continuum of experience from its controlling ground in the spatio-temporal structures of the real world, so that it can be perceived and enjoyed in its pure and vivid sensuous impression. It is understandable that when the natural pattern of appearances begins to break up and fall apart, artificial devices are often brought in to give them some meaningful coherent integration, which is what one finds taking place in certain abstract art.

Emerging from the Cultural Split

What I have been describing holds true across the whole range of human experience, in any field of study or inquiry in which we seek to give an account of what we perceive and apprehend in sets of coherent and meaningful statements. Let us take as an example the scientific investigation of some particular reality, in which our discoveries involve us in propounding a scientific theory about it, or at least in making a set of controlled and orderly statements about it. They are statements that we develop out of our empirical relation to the reality concerned, and of course they have to be consistent with one another or logically coherent—otherwise they would not make sense. But if they are to be scientifically meaningful they must refer to that reality in terms of what it is independently of our thought or our statement about it. It is that objective or ontological reference that is primary; without it all that is said would ultimately be empty and meaningless, for it would fail of its intention. All scientific thought and statement, and all rational thought and statement, are pivoted primarily upon ontological references—which also applies to sets of statements in their coherent formations with each other. It is through the semantic interconnection of the ontological reference and the coherence of our statements that they fulfill their true function in scientific and rational knowledge. This is precisely the way we think and speak of things in our ordinary experience and communication in daily life—scientific operations are only a rigorous extension of that.

Suppose, however, that the ontological relation of a set of statements to the realities to which they are meant to refer is cut or damaged—suppose the objective reference is suspended—what are you to make of them? What meaning are you to give to such statements? How are you to interpret them? There are, apparently, only two alternatives. *Either* you interpret them by reference to the subject who made them, in which case they are to be understood as forms of his life, expressive of the states of his consciousness or the attitude of mind he takes up—and if it relates to his experience as an observer, they cannot refer to things as they are but only to their appearances: that is, to the impressions they make on him or to what they mean for him. *Or* you interpret them in terms of the interrelations of the statements with one another, by penetrating through linguistic analysis into their grammatical and logical structure, in which case you are confined to their syntactical meaning, for with the breaking of their objective or ontological reference, the semantic focus of statements collapses on itself.

Consider what happens when this state of affairs obtains in philosophy. *Either* you are confined to a form of existentialism in which the statements concerned are understood to express your attitude to existence—or, for example, what your attitude to the other world means for you here and now—for the focus of attention throughout is upon self-understanding, and only upon what is other than you insofar as it provokes or elicits deeper self-understanding on your part. *Or* you are confined to some kind of language philosophy that restricts itself to the analysis and clarification of linguistic and logical connections, and to the discussion of classical philosophical problems transposed onto that formal basis, bracketed off from metaphysical considerations that have to do with the bearing of thought and statement upon being. While existentialism has much to say about being, it does not admit of any concept of the *logos* inherent in being; being, therefore, cannot be known in its inner relations. Thus existentalism remains trapped in the Kantian dualism. On the other hand, the various forms of language philosophy took their rise from the positivist and nominalist views of science advocated by Ernst Mach (who insisted that scientific theories can have no claim to bear upon being), so that in their radical rejection of metaphysics, they also remain trapped in the Kantian dualism and its denial of any knowledge of things in their internal relations. Existentialism and language philosophy are evidently twin errors that arise from the basic error of such a radical break in the ontological reference of our concepts and statements to reality that there is automatically ruled out of consideration the Einsteinian understanding of basic scientific knowledge as grasping reality in its depth or as the apprehension of the intelligibility inherent in the universe independent of our perceiving of it. That is why scientists who are engaged in penetrating into the objective structures and intrinsic intelligibilities of the universe can have little to do with the philosophies of existentialism and linguistic analysis, for these philosophies are irrelevant to the rational understanding of the real world.

It does not take much to see that the same twin errors can and do arise in people's handling of theological statements within the same dualist framework. Take such statements as "The Word was made flesh," "God is love," "God was in Christ, reconciling the world to himself." If the objective reference of these statements, which is clearly intended by the biblical witness, is cut off, as is demanded by a deistic disjunction between God and the world—which makes the "act" of God at best only one that is tangential to our world without intersecting it—then what do we have? On the one hand, such statements may be interpreted in a subjective and anthropocentric way with reference to the consciousness of the agents of the tradition or the biblical writers, so that their objective form is only a mythological way of expressing man's feeling of dependence on God and the understanding of himself in the world in which he lives. Thus, theological statements about God are turned round into being statements about ourselves as dependent on God; and theological statements about Jesus Christ are turned round into being statements about the meaning he has for us in our freedom to be ourselves and to live a life of self-commitment in faith and love. All this has the reductionist effect of transposing transcendent—or, as it were, vertical—reference to God or Christ into purely immanent or horizontal reference, in which relations with God and Christ are converted into interrelations between persons on a purely mundane level. On the other hand, theological statements may be treated as logical propositions to be analyzed and interpreted in their syntactical and coherent interrelations: which may lead in a fundamentalist direction, in which people are concerned mainly with the relation of statement to statement in a formalistic elision of the truth of being with the truth of statement, or may lead in a nominalist direction, in which theological doctrines—as they disintegrate in their detachment from the empirical and objective ground in the acts of God, and are thus made void of material content—are shown to be meaningless. Whichever way we look at it, these ways of handling theological statements reveal what happens when we reject, as Bultmann frankly does, any conception of "the intelligibility of reality": our thoughts and statements then derive from no objective source and point to nothing beyond ourselves—they are ultimately no more than autobiographical statements, and theology inevitably degenerates into anthropology (and not very good anthropology at that).

Let me now sharpen this account of the effect of dualism upon theology by considering what happens to our understanding of Christ. The dualist paradigms of thought with which people operate have the double effect of detaching Jesus Christ from God, on the one hand, and of detaching the message of Jesus Christ from his person, on the other hand. Here then we have an uprooting of Jesus from his ground in the Being of God, and an uprooting of Jesus' teaching and message from its intrinsic relation to his personal Being. Now it is this detachment of Jesus from God and detachment of the teaching of Jesus from his Person that have given rise to so much of the confusion current in the convictions of Christian people. Yet this state of affairs is not new.

Let us recall that when the Christian Gospel was proclaimed in the ancient world and Christian thought began to be disseminated in society and culture, they had to be expressed and communicated to people in a world of deeply entrenched dualist thought. In the background, of course, there was the dualism of Greek philosophy and science, which we considered earlier; but the dualism in religion with which Christian theology had to struggle was of two sorts. On the one hand, there was the very radical dualism, held by the Gnostic sects on the fringe of the Church, between two widely disparate realms: a suprasensual, utterly transcendental realm of eternal and divine realities and a very earthy, material realm of transient and murky existence—the gap between them was so wide that it had to be spanned through mythological hierarchies of semidivine beings. On the other hand, there was another form of dualism, found in the Arian movement of thought within the Church, according to which the disparate realms of the uncreated and divine and of the creaturely and human touched each other, but only tangentially at a sort of mathematical point that they identified with Jesus. And he, they held, belonged ultimately to this world of created being and not to the other world of divine Being, although he was reckoned to be the first of created realities, called the Word, or Son of God, through whom the rest of creation was related to the Creator.

Now it was in the impact of those dualisms upon Christian theology that we have the rise of demythologizing, and of what one might call philosophical mythologizing. In the Gnostic view, the two worlds are so utterly separated from one another that any thought of interaction between them or any idea of an incursion of elements of the other world into this world had to be understood, not in a real, but only in a mythological way. Thus, their radical dualism made Gnostics regard the biblical account of the acts of God in history, or of the incarnation, crucifixion, and resurrection of the Son of God in space and time, as myths. Instead of merely rejecting them, however, they sought to make spiritual sense of those myths for themselves by giving them a "gnostic" or "high-flown philosophical" interpretation. That is the philosophical mythologization that one finds among semi-Christian Gnostics in the second and third centuries. In the Arian view, on the other hand, although the two worlds are utterly disparate, the other world of God bears upon this world—not in such a way that it intersects or overlaps it, however, but in such a way that it impinges upon it at a timeless and spaceless changing point. This form of dualism required them to de-mythologize the Christian faith, in the sense that because Jesus belongs ultimately only to this world of created and changeable realities and not also to the world of unchanging divine reality, he can be understood only as the symbol and not as the downright reality in space and time of the time-less, unchanging reality of God. Jesus Christ is to be treated, therefore, as a detached and changeable image of God and cannot be invested with the finality and determi-nate character of one whose being is grounded in the eternal and unique Being of God. He is only an intermediary and is not himself the unique Mediator between God and man who bridges divine and human being in his own Person. On such a unitarian view of God there could ultimately be no place for trinitarian theology.

In the face of that dualist outlook in religion and thought invading the Church from the surrounding culture of the ancient world, what line did classical Christian the-ology take? It was committed to the Gospel of the incarna-tion of the Son of God, the Word made flesh, and was con-cerned with a way of believing and thinking imposed upon it by the sheer fact of Christ, in accordance with which it was held that this world of ours in space and time is actu-ally intersected and overlapped, so to speak, by the divine world in the *parousia*, or advent and presence, of Jesus Christ. He was acknowledged and adored, therefore, as one who is God of God and yet man of man, who in his own being belongs both to the eternal world of divine reality and to the historical world of contingent realities. The linchpin of this theology, the essential bond of connection that held it together in its foundations, as it was formulated in the great ecumenical creed of all Christendom at Nicaea and Constantinople, is the so-called *homoousion*, the confession that Jesus Christ the incarnate Son is of one being or of one substance with God the Father. Because Jesus Christ is God of God and man of man in himself, in Christ we who are creatures of this world may know God in such a way that our knowledge of him rests upon the reality of God himself. It is not something that is thought up and devised out of ourselves and mythologically projected into God, but it is grounded and controlled by what God is in himself.

The Nicene theology thus gave basic shape to the doctrine of the Trinity that was found to belong to the essential structure of faith in God and to the intrinsic grammar of Christian thought. If Jesus Christ is in his own being what he is as God's revealing word and saving act toward us, or if, conversely, what God is toward us in the revealing word and saving act of Christ, he is inherently in his own eternal Being, then through Christ and in one Spirit we are given access to God as he is in himself. If the revealing word and the saving act of the incarnate Son are not external but internal to the Being of God, then we are given, in some measure at least, knowledge of God in his internal relations as Father, Son and Holy Spirit. All-important here is the epistemological force of the *homoousion*, or the consubstantial relation between Jesus Christ the Word made flesh and God himself, for the mediation of knowledge of God in his intrinsic reality and intelligibility. Moreover, if Jesus Christ in his word and act is the image of God, identical with his reality, the imaging of God in his incarnate life on earth has a place of unique and controlling finality in our knowledge of God. If Jesus Christ is the one place in space and time where we may really know the Father, then God the Father made known to us through him cannot be some static, immutable, impassible Deity utterly remote from us, but the dynamic, living God, whose Being is inherent in his Word and Act and whose Word and Act are inherent in the unity of his Being, and who has locked himself with us in our being and destiny in Jesus Christ our Brother.

Quite clearly, this formulation of the Christian doctrine of God could not have developed without a reconstruction of the dualist foundations of ancient Greek and Roman culture in philosophy, science, and religion. That is indeed what Christian theology carried out in the early centuries of the Christian era, into which we shall probe in the next lecture. Thus, the foundations of classical Christian theology were laid and given credal formulation in the process of overcoming the dualist modes of thought that threatened to undermine the Gospel and to paganize the Church.

In our own times, as I have been trying to show throughout this lecture, Christian theology has been struggling once more with dualist modes of thought that drive a wedge between Christ and God, and correspondingly between the message of Christ and Christ himself—for in detachment from God, Christ is no longer a figure of final and intrinsic significance. The result of all this is that, not Christ, but some kind of Christianity detached from Christ becomes the focus of people's attention and the religion of our Churches. Such a detached Christian religion cannot exist by itself, and cultural status and meaning for it must be found in human life; and so it inevitably becomes attached to human society, where it becomes the object of phenomenological and sociological analysis and study. But in this event it suffers even more acutely from the abstraction of the phenomenological surface of our experience from its objective grounds in reality, and from the disintegration of form that follows from that. Thus it is inevitably trapped in the fragmentation and disruption of our so-called pluralist society and its split culture. It is not surprising that in this state of affairs we find rife in avant-garde theology modern forms of Gnosticism and Arianism that can be paralleled at point after point with their ancient counterparts, or that this revival of long-discarded heresies should point Christian theology back to the Nicene era for its cue in the renewed battle for the essence of the Gospel.

However, we are in a much more fortunate position today than the Early Church, for our modern world is one in which dualist modes of thought have already been destroyed in the advance of scientific knowledge and its transition to integrated outlook upon the universe in the rediscovered unity of form and being, or of structure and substance. This remains valid throughout the whole range of human knowledge, wherever we have to do with the interrelation of theoretical and empirical factors. The old epistemological, cosmological, and religious dualisms that underlie the strange modern revival of Gnostic and Arian thought are shown to be without any force. The same applies to the epistemological, phenomenological, and deistic dualisms that evidently underpin the revival of nineteenth-century theologies, notably those of Schleiermacher and Ritschl, for in every field of inquiry we establish genuine knowledge in terms of its internal relations and intelligibility—the very points that were and still are being denied by Kantian and Heideggerian forms of philosophy. The difference that has come about can be vividly indicated by pointing to the debate between Ernst Mach and Max Planck in quantum theory over the question of the reality of atoms. Mach claimed that atoms do not have any existence in reality and are no more than symbols that we use in the theoretical conventions of physics, for it is impossible to know things in their internal relations. But of course we can, and it is precisely by penetrating into the internal structure of atoms that physics has made such startling advance in our knowledge of nature, but in so doing it destroyed the Kantian and Machian thesis that phenomenological knowledge was restricted to external relations or appearances.

That is the revolution that has been going on in recent decades in the very foundations of scientific knowledge, but its effect has yet to be felt in its full force throughout the human sciences—especially in the social sciences, which still lag far behind, but not least in biblical and theological inquiry. But the split culture that derives from the old dualisms is itself steadily being undermined as new integrative modes of thought from below take over and affect the surface patterns of our culture. In this transitional period interdisciplinary study and dialogue can be of the greatest service, but in the last analysis it will be, above all, the dialogue between theological and natural science that will play the most effective role, for through it there will surely emerge a new openness to the creative impact of God, the unifying Source of all rational order and beauty in the universe.

3

Creation and Science

I N MY LAST LECTURE I spoke of the fact that many of our
contemporaries are afraid of relating theology and science, and I suggested that what lies behind that fear is a
false view of science as well as a false view of theology. If
science is equated merely with instrumentalist science or
technology—How do we master and manipulate nature for
our own ends?—then how can that way of thinking be applied to God? And that is a good question. But how can
you base theology on science? That is a question people
keep on asking me, and that too is a good question, especially if science is of the instrumentalist or technological
sort. In the last lecture, I tried to show that the whole picture has altered, for a new world has opened up, involving
basic changes in science, and even determinism has been
disposed of, or at least relativized, for it holds good only at
a comparatively low level of reality and then only within
certain severe limits. Today I want to show that far from
theology being based on natural science, the opposite, if
anything, is nearer the truth!

CREATION AND SCIENCE

The deeper that scientific inquiry probes, the more it is clear that in science we are concerned to penetrate into the intrinsic structures of the universe in such a way that its basic *design* becomes disclosed. Hence we are forced to grapple with cosmological questions and to adopt a fundamental attitude to the universe as a whole: a *Weltbild*—not a *Weltanschauung*, which is a naturalistic attitude, but a *Weltbild*. Now natural science cannot be pursued without being committed to a fundamental attitude to the world, which affects all theory and all theory-laden experiment. In theological science, on the other hand, we are concerned, as I shall show later in more detail, not just with God/man relations, but with God/man/world or God/world/man relations, so that an understanding of the *world* enters into the coefficients of theological concepts and statements. Theological science cannot be pursued scientifically without being committed to a fundamental attitude to the world, for theological concepts without empirical correlates in our world of space and time would be empty and irrelevant for us. Hence the more rigorously we pursue science today, and the more rigorously we pursue our theology, the more we find there breaking out an inevitable and proper dialogue between theological science and natural science, if only because both have to develop fundamental attitudes to the world.

I would like to demonstrate that by looking again at the Early Church, where we have the rise of classical theology—and by classical theology I mean the Nicene theology and all that followed in the next two centuries—when, especially in Greek theology, we have the foundations of the theology upon which all Christendom rests and to which all our Creeds go back. In this period in the Early

Church we find Christian theology struggling to break through the pagan outlook upon the world with its identification of cosmology and theology, and often the identification of God and the world. There were Stoic thinkers, for example, who held that God was the soul of the world, animating it and giving it motion much as the human soul does to the body. In this way theology and cosmology were bound together. It is much the same with Aristotle's finite view of God as the unmoved Mover of the finite universe, and so it was natural for him to include theology under the rubric of "cosmology." There was bound to be a mighty confrontation in the early centuries between the Judeo-Christian understanding of God as the transcendent Lord of the universe and the fatalistic outlook upon God and the universe in Greco-Roman thought and religion—especially between the revelation of the one God as Creator of earth and heaven and of all things visible and invisible, and the dualist structures of the ancient world, with their bifurcation between what is real and eternal and changeless and what is unreal, apparent, and evanescent. Think, for example, of the Old Testament concept of the living God who interacts through his Word and Spirit providentially and savingly with the world he has made, with its emphasis on the one hand upon the reality and goodness of God to his creatures and on the other hand upon the reality and goodness of the world he has created. Here, then, we have a contrast between the God as the mighty living and active source of all that is good and real and orderly and the God who is statically and timelessly changeless—bound up with the eternal forms that constitute the nature of ultimate reality or the inertial source of all the immanent processes in the universe, regularly identified in literature with fate or necessity, and therefore also with the evil as well as the good that overtakes the world and all the inexorable processes within it. There was thus a head-on clash at essential points in the basic structures of thought.

However, it was particularly when Christianity came upon the scene everywhere—with its doctrine of the overwhelming love of God, of creation out of nothing, and its doctrines of the incarnation and the resurrection, according to which the interaction of God with the world takes on the form of the advent and presence of God himself in Jesus Christ within the space-time structures of created existence—that the clash reached its greatest intensity. With Christianity we have continued, of course, the Judaic emphasis upon the goodness and reality of the created world, as the handiwork of the good God, which is not to be denigrated or despised, and which is not to be treated as merely transient and evanescent, for it is bound up with the eternal purpose of God and his untiring faithfulness. In the sharp form that this took in Christian theology, there could be no compromise with the pagan view of God and the world. What was required was a radical reconstruction of the foundations of ancient philosophy, science, and culture, for only as it was able to succeed in doing that was the Christian Gospel able to take root in the civilized world and to transform its society until it was brought within the Kingdom of Christ.

Now pause for a little to contrast that reconstruction with what has been happening in our own times. Today Christian thought tends to be expounded within the patterns of thought and even the transient fashions of contemporary culture. Thomas S. Kuhn, in his widely known book *The Structures of Scientific Revolutions*, has shown that while the scientist is normally concerned with developing his thought within certain ongoing paradigms pervading the community or society in which he lives, whenever he undertakes any creative thought—as in the major discoveries and advances of science—he leaps ahead of the thought-world of society and develops new concepts that are in fundamental conflict with the paradigms of the community and that cannot be assimilated to them without a revolutionary change or conversion. It is only as the new concepts alter the paradigmatic structures of people's thought that science can establish its major advances. Now regarded from this point of view, it must be admitted that modern theology has been acting in the opposite way. Instead of trying to change the paradigms of society and culture, whole generations of preachers, scholars, and theologians have been asking how they can communicate the Gospel and make it understandable and relevant to the modern world, and in answer they have been trying to fit the Christian message to the paradigms of the community—otherwise, they argue, people today would not understand what Christianity is about. Thus, while science advances through changing our thought, the preaching and teaching of the Church become more and more obsolescent. Is that not why, in the last few decades, the more we have tried to make the Gospel relevant, the more it has become irrelevant to our contemporaries, while theology has fallen into the deep fissures that have opened up in our split culture?

But when we look back to the Early Church, and think of the staggering conquest of the ancient world by the Galilean, we find that this took place precisely as early Christian theology—instead of trying merely to operate within the paradigms of the ancient pagan world—undertook the enormous task of recreating the very foundations of human philosophy, science, and culture so that the Gospel could take deep root and develop within human society in such a way as to evangelize and convert it, and would thus fulfill its own cultural role in clarifying and unifying all human knowledge and life under the creative impact of God's self-revelation in Christ and the ordering power of his love. In that process it was particularly the Christian teaching about the incarnation (including the passion and resurrection of Christ) in its relation to the creation that brought the Church into conflict with the prevailing outlook and forced it to develop an ordered outlook of a distinctively Christian orientation upon the whole relation of God to the universe, which shook the ancient world to its foundations and called for new ways of human life and religious belief.

It was in the course of this development that proper theology arose, and by *proper theology* I mean "dogmatics." Let me explain this. In the ancient world the schools of Plato and Aristotle were succeeded by the so-called "New Academy," in which philosophers (who soon came to be called "skeptics") concentrated on asking questions and questions and questions, but were not prepared to entertain positive answers—the kind of questions that people so often ask in the ecumenical movement: that is to say, questions that do not yield the kind of answers that commit you to decision and change. And of course we still dub questions of that sort merely "academic questions." But in the last two centuries before Christ and in the first two centuries after Christ there arose philosophers of a different kind—initiating a movement of thought that in some respects was the precursor of empirical science—who were nicknamed, by the superior people who ask only academic questions the "dogmatics" because they devoted themselves to questions yielding positive answers and thus to inquiries leading to real and useful knowledge. These "dogmatics" claimed that they were concerned, not with abstract and useless questions, but with questions about the actual world around them and with the kind of answers forced upon them by the nature of things, which they could not refrain from accepting and acting upon. Thus the "dogmatic" person turns out to be, not a philosopher, but a scientist who thinks only as he is compelled to think by the objective and intrinsic structures of nature.

This was a movement of thought that the Christian theologians took up and developed, changing it and its foundations through relating the intrinsic structures of nature to God's creation out of nothing. This is what Cyril of Alexandria called *dogmatike episteme*, "dogmatic science," and he applied the term to Christian theology. And this is indeed the kind of theology we find in the great Councils of the Church—not some kind of theological freethinking, but the kind of theology of God and Christ that is forced upon us by the actual interaction of God with the universe he has made and by his intelligible self-revelation within that interaction. As we allow our minds to fall under the power of what we hear and find there, we find ourselves committed to saying fundamental things about God and the world, Christ and the Spirit, and the Church. Thus there arose dogmatic science or theology, developing certain basic ideas that changed the whole course of science. That is what I wish to speak about today.

But before I do so, let me point to the fact that the term *dogmatic* has changed its use in our common parlance and tends to have a sense opposite to its original use. To be dogmatic in this more modern sense means to be the kind of person who lays down certain definite ideas and propositions apart from any controlling evidential grounds and merely under the constraint of external authorities and preconceptions—traditional, ecclesiastical, political, or even scientistic—but these ideas are not ideas and propositions forced on us by the objective structures of reality. *Dogmatic* in this sense came, unfortunately, to be applied to the propositions and doctrines of the Church. Now it is worth noting that at the beginnings of modern science in its empirical form, it sometimes applied to itself the word *dogmatic*, but in its classical and not its vulgar sense. Taking their cue from Francis Bacon, for example, scientists insisted they did not want to have anything to do with academic questions or the questions of the philosophers, for they could not help them to understand nature or to discover new knowledge that would advance science—rather like the sort of thing that scientists today say about the linguistic philosophy when they claim that they cannot learn anything from this sort of formalistic and academic questioning and analysis. Science needs questions of the interrogatory kind—in which nature is allowed to disclose itself and in which science is allowed to discern nature's inner form and order, which it seeks to bring to controlled expression. Laws of nature are thus the dogmas that are imposed on the scientific mind by the immanent rationality of the universe, just as crystalline formations impose upon our thinking the geometric patterns embedded in them. In order to distinguish this from medieval science or from the approach of the philosophers, scientists gave to physics the name of "dogmatic science." It is in that tradition, then, that Reformation theology (especially in the Lutheran and Reformed Churches and universities)—recovering the outlook of patristic thought—developed its understanding of theology as "dogmatic science," or "Christian dogmatics," to distinguish it from some other dogmatic science like physics. It is in that meaning of the term that I have tried to profess Christian dogmatics at the University of Edinburgh.

To return to my main argument then: in its reconstruction of the foundations of ancient philosophy, science, and culture, Christian theology of this rigorous dogmatic sort in the Early Church developed three masterful ideas, overlapping each other, that have had a powerful effect on all subsequent thought, in natural science as well as in theological science. They arose, as I said earlier, out of careful thinking together of the doctrines of the incarnation of the eternal *Logos* and of the creation of the world out of nothing.

1) The first of these ideas is what we may call the *rational unity of the universe*. This is something we have come to accept so readily—largely owing to our great medieval inheritance—that we hardly realize that it is a distinctively Judeo-Christian concept. Behind this idea lies the doctrine of the one God, the Creator of all things visible and invisible, the Creator of the rational forms (to use the Greek expression) as well as the matter of things, and who as such is the ultimate Source of all order and rationality in the universe. This carries with it the rejection of all polytheism, dualism, pluralism, and polymorphism of ancient religions, philosophies, and science, and produces the concept of one harmonious system of things characterized by one pervasive, if multi-variable, unity in the universe. If

you want to get the clearest grasp of what this means, study the *Contra Gentes* of St. Athanasius and see how again and again he employs musical terms to describe the kind of symphonic texture that the order of the universe under one God the Creator has. It is this masterful idea of a unified rationality that sweeps away the Aristotelian, the Neoplatonic, and certainly the Ptolemaic duality between celestial and terrestrial worlds, celestial and terrestrial mechanics, and all the dualism and pluralism that go with it, for this universe as it comes from the creative Word of God has one pervading *taxis*, or order, everywhere, so that wherever you go in the universe it is accessible to rational inquiry. Now that is a correlate to the doctrine of the one God who created the universe out of nothing, and it is upon that idea of the rationality or intelligibility of the universe that the confidence of all scientific inquiry has rested ever since.

2) The idea of the *contingent rationality or intelligibility of the universe*. This registers another immense step forward, although it was considered to be even more difficult. The idea that the rationality of the universe is contingent, i.e., neither necessary nor eternal, that there is an order in the universe created—along with the universe—out of nothing, was quite impossible for Greeks and Orientals alike. Again and again when Christians taught the doctrine of creation out of nothing, they were met with accusations of "impiety." It was, they were told, a form of atheism, for it called in question the rationality of the eternal forms—and denied the necessary connection between the rationality immanent in things and its source in Deity whether Deity was conceived in a Platonic, Aristotelian, or Stoic way— and it undermined the stability of the natural principles

informing all that is, without which there would be nothing to stand between cosmos and chaos. It is certainly understandable that from the Greek point of view, this Christian idea should be regarded with such horror, but nevertheless it did prevail and it took root along with the victory over Greek polytheism achieved by the monotheistic concept of God.

Let us consider the notion of contingent rationality more closely. In creating the universe out of nothing, God created space and time out of nothing as well, for they came to be along with the creation as immanent functions within the universe. On the one hand, this doctrine of creation changed the basic understanding of space and time—destroying the container concept applied to their understanding in different ways by Platonic, Aristotelian, and Stoic philosophy—and replaced it with a relational concept. This represents one of the greatest changes imaginable, and it is indeed a change with which we have only managed to catch up in our own day, with relativity theory. The relational notions of space and time developed by theology were then translated into physics by John Philoponos of Alexandria, whose work later had some influence in the West through Al Ghazali and Grosseteste—but we need not pursue that here. On the other hand, since space and time are the bearers of rational order within the universe, the creation of space and time out of nothing meant that the rational order immanent in the universe is created out of nothing. That was as I have said, a staggering concept for the ancient world, but there is more to come.

The creation of the world out of nothing means that man, endowed as he is with mind as well as soul and body, is also created out of nothing, and that means that the human mind is created out of nothing. That was certainly an extremely difficult idea for the Greeks to swallow, for all Greek thought and religion were somehow informed by the Orphic idea that the mind or the intelligence is a spark of the divine—how many people today hold this pagan idea as well!—so that for them the light of the reason could no more be considered to be created out of nothing than could God. For Christians, however, the Greek view led to the divinization of the creature—which detracted from the glory and majesty and truth of God himself while damaging the true status of the creature. Thus Christian theology, while rejecting dualism, operated with a distinction between created and uncreated light, or created and uncreated rationality—the former deriving from the latter, but not as an extension or emanation of it—which had the effect of maintaining the creaturely integrity of the creature and the human integrity of man.

In creating man, endowed with mind as well as with soul and body, out of nothing, God created within the universe an intelligent counterpart to the rational order immanent in the creation through the functioning of space and time. By positing the human intelligence along with space and time in his creation of the universe out of nothing, God conferred upon it a rationality of its own, independent of, yet contingent upon, his own uncreated and transcendent rationality. This does not mean that the rationality of the universe is a sharing in God, or that the created light of the human mind is an "ontologistic" participation in the mind of God—as, for example, Neoplatonists seemed to think. On the contrary, while as created light it derives from the uncreated light of God, it is independent of it yet by no means self-sufficient—as God's light is. By its very nature as created and contingent, it points away from itself to the uncreated light and in its creaturely way reflects it. This is the doctrine of contingent intelligibility inherent in the creation, which means that if you are to understand any natural process in the universe, you cannot do so by any *a priori* thought, or by any kind of theological reasoning from what we know of God, but only by going to the natural process itself and probing into its natural or intrinsic order. The contingence of the universe means that it might not have been, or might well have been other than it is, so that we must ask our questions of the universe itself if we are to understand it—that is the reason why we cannot do without experimental science, which is the appropriate way of questioning nature. But the contingent universe is intelligible—endowed with a rationality of its own—so that if we are to understand the universe, we must probe into that intelligibility, which is the immanent language by means of which the universe answers our questions or experiments. Thus it becomes apparent that the doctrine of contingent intelligibility or rationality is the foundation of all empirical and theoretical science, while the essential connection between "contingence" and "intelligibility" means that in all our science we have to operate with an indissoluble connection between empirical and theoretical factors, both in what we seek to know and in our knowing of it. Today general relativity and the singularity of the universe so astonishingly disclosed by modern cosmology provide massive support for this masterful idea as never before in the history of science. Yet this idea, which was quite impossible for the pagan mind, is a direct product of Christian theology. It is evident from this alone that far from theology being grounded upon natural science, natural science rests for one of its most basic concepts upon Christian theology.

3) The idea of *the freedom of the universe*, that is, its *contingent freedom*. Behind this lies a powerful conception of the freedom of God, which stems from the deep background of the Church in Judaic thought, but which Christian theologians energetically developed in the course of their struggle with Greek thought, in order to divorce theology from cosmology. As the Creator of the whole cosmos out of nothing, God is the transcendent Lord over all space and time. He is not indebted to the universe in any way or bound to it by some sort of dualist synthesis such as monistic philosophy or pantheistic religion evidently entailed. The universe is indebted to God and utterly dependent on him, both in its origin and in its continuity. Its rationality, the regularity of its ongoing order, is indebted to his rationality, but God's rationality is not indebted to the universe. He does not need the universe to be God. He is majestically and almightily free over all created existence, and in that sense he was often spoken of as "superessential" or "beyond being," i.e., beyond created being. Yet God's freedom is not arbitrary freedom, for almighty though he is, he is, in his own transcendent Being, intrinsically and supremely rational, and as such is the transcendent Source of all truth, rationality, and order in the universe.

It is because it is contingent upon that God and his freedom that the universe cannot be regarded as enslaved in any way to some kind of alien power or destiny. Hence the doctrine of the freedom of the universe grounded in the freedom of God helped to emancipate people's minds from the tyranny of fate, necessity, and determinism that pagan thought had clamped down upon the world through the conception of the inexorably cyclic processes of a self-sufficient, closed universe. This is very evident in the attempts of early Christian thinkers such as Clement or Athanasius of Alexandria or Athenagoras of Athens to lift the concept of *pronoia*, or divine providence, on to an altogether higher level, for it was the Judeo-Christian concept of the providence of God manifested in creating and preserving the world—and in redeeming triumph over the forces of evil and disorder—that was so effective in destroying the fatalistic outlook upon things derived from the deadening idea of a universe shackled to unending recurrence and harnessed to an altogether necessitarian and blind destiny. This has nowhere been more fully or effectively shown than by Stanley L. Jaki in two recent works, *Science and Creation* and *The Road of Science and the Ways of God*. The doctrine of creation out of nothing and of the continual preservation of creation from lapsing back into nothing, shattered the notion of eternal cyclic processes, with its built-in futility, for it revealed that the universe had an absolute beginning and thus replaced the idea of time ever turning back on itself with an linear view of time moving irreversibly toward its consummation or end in the purpose of the Creator. But it also grounded the ongoing order of the universe in the steadfast love and faithfulness of God, which gave it a stability as well as freedom in its contingency, for it meant that its natural lability was undergirded by God himself.

The contingent freedom of the universe, then, is not something bound up with randomness or chance, for it is no more arbitrary than the freedom of the God of infinite love and truth upon which it rests and by which it is maintained. It is a freedom that derives from the unlimited freedom of God, but it is a contingent freedom and is therefore a limited freedom. An unlimited contingent freedom would be an inherent contradiction—that would spell arbitrariness. Limited though contingent freedom is, it is limited by the very freedom of God on which it is grounded. It is nonetheless a genuine freedom, the kind of freedom proper to a finite and contingent universe. On the other hand, because it is contingent upon the unlimited freedom of God, it is a freedom that embraces inexhaustible possibilities. That is why as we explore the universe in our scientific activities, it keeps on surprising us, disclosing to us patterns and structures in an indefinite range of intelligibility, which we could never anticipate on our own—such is the excitement of scientific enterprise. Indeed, it is the hallmark of a true scientific theory in its bearing upon reality that it indicates far more than it can express, so that the more we probe through it into the intelligibilities of the universe, the more exciting are the aspects and forms of reality that become disclosed to us. The universe constantly takes us by surprise in this way because it is correlated to the infinite, inexhaustible freedom and rationality of God, its Creator. It is understandable, therefore, that Christian theology should think of the creation as grounded upon the grace of God, for grace is the free love of God, which always takes us by surprise. And it is also understandable that natural scientists like Michael Polanyi should suggest that reality may well be defined in terms of its power for manifesting itself in unthought-of and unanticipated ways in the future. It is certainly in respect of its contingent freedom as well as its contingent intelligibility that the universe disclosed to

[59

us by modern scientific inquiry stands out more and more as an open universe that we may grasp and describe only through open structures of thought.

It was, then, in terms of these masterful ideas that classical Christian theology of the fourth, fifth, and sixth centuries worked out its outlook upon the universe and at the same time reconstructed the cultural foundations in philosophy and science upon which the pagan picture of God and the cosmos rested. Time does not allow me to show how these three ideas developed in Christian theology or how they came to shape the Christian outlook upon God and the world that informs the great Creeds. Nor is there time to discuss the attempts that were made to translate these ideas from the idiom of theology into the idiom of physics, notably by John Philoponos of Alexandria, to whom I have already referred. He was the first Christian physicist, who, following upon the theological work of Athanasius and Cyril in Alexandria, developed a physics of light—and in that same connection, a new concept of motion—as well as relational notions of space and time, which are an astonishing anticipation of our own scientific notions today. The profound interconnection revealed there between theology and science in respect to these basic ideas was, as it were, a prophecy of what was to follow in the subsequent history of thought, but at no time has that interconnection been more evident than it is today.

Now what became of these masterful ideas? Unfortunately, they became submerged in a massive upsurge of dualist modes of thought and the container notions of space in East and West, in Byzantine and Latin Christian cultures. To a large extent this was due to the powerful influence of Neoplatonic philosophy, with its reinterpretation of Plato and Aristotle (not least Aristotle's logic), and the survival of dualist Stoic notions of law in the development of canon law. All the way through the fifth, sixth, and seventh centuries when the great theological and scientific reconstruction was going on, the old dualisms operated below the surface, corroding the new ideas (not least those of John Philoponos), and then broke out into the open and were given paradigmatic status in the West through the subtle but admittedly beautiful blending of Christian theology with Neoplatonic philosophy and Ptolemaic cosmology by the great St. Augustine. Already, however, a somewhat dualist understanding of Christology, which took its cue from Leo's famous *Tome* to the Council of Chalcedon, provided the platform from which the views of John Philoponos were rejected as "monophysite" and heretical. A monophysite is someone who denies that there are two "natures"—a divine and human nature—in Christ, where *nature* is interpreted in an Aristotelian way. For John Philoponos, however, who did not think in an Aristotelian way, in line with the theological and scientific tradition to which he belonged, *nature* meant "reality," so that for him to think of Christ as "one nature" meant that he was "one reality," and not a schizoid being. John Philoponos was no monophysite in the heretical sense, but the accusation of heresy had the effect of denigrating also his anti-dualist thought in science and philosophy. This represents, in my view, one of the greatest tragedies in the history of science as well as of theology, for it really means that the Church was ultimately unwilling to work out in the rigorous way required the distinctively Christian ideas of the relation between God and the world. By remaining content with Conciliar theology and by concentrating on administration and law, the Church remained trapped in the continuity of the insufficiently tamed dualist patterns of thought embedded in Greco-Roman culture and popular Christian religion, and it even invited those dualist patterns of thought to take over. Thus, the great advances in Alexandrian science, and the extensive interconnection between science and theology worked out there, were largely lost, if only because in the Augustinian dualist outlook this world of space and time has no ultimate place in the Christian hope, but belongs to the world that passes away—that is, the world out of which we must be saved.

I have said that the revolutionary ideas introduced by Christian theology into the foundations of our scientific outlook upon the universe became submerged, but the doctrine of the one God—with its correlate in the unitary rationality of the universe—remained and indeed received considerable attention and development in Latin medieval thought, which played its due part in the emergence of modern science. The medieval outlook had its problems, for it incorporated the Ptolemaic cosmology—with its hard separation between celestial and terrestrial motion—which had to be radically questioned before modern astronomy and science could take their rise based on a unitary physics spanning the heavenly bodies and the earth. Nevertheless, medieval theology and philosophy realized that something had to be done to close the gap between the concept of the rationality pervading this world that comes from God and the Neoplatonic-Ptolemaic dualism embedded in its Augustinian religion and culture, otherwise Christianity would become so otherworldly that every aspect of the Church's life and work throughout its earthly pilgrimage could be given only a mystical-symbolic interpretation. Thus, they reinterpreted the loose idea of the sacramental universe (inherited from St. Augustine) through the media of resurrected Aristotelian concepts correlating form and matter, but stressing the conception of form, identified with the rational soul, as the final determination of matter in the process of becoming. This was a thoroughly teleological understanding of the universe, which could be integrated with and could modify Augustinian eschatology and its world-denying outlook. Such a synthesis, however, while it performed magnificent service—the fruit of which is seen in medieval art, and in architecture as well as in philosophy—gave rise to intractable theological and scientific difficulties bound up with the notion of God as the Unmoved Mover or Final Cause of motion in man and nature. God is thus thought of as "acting" in the world only indirectly, by way of inducing in its latent activity a change from a state of potentiality to a state of actuality. This introduced into Christian theology a covert Aristotelian type of deism that so damaged the theistic understanding of the living interaction between God and the world at crucial points such as the incarnation and the real presence as to call for rather artificial explanatory concepts, and also introduced into the scientific outlook on the world a logico-causal systematization of nature that was to inhibit the development of empirical science.

This medieval synthesis certainly had the satisfactory effect of reinforcing the conception of the objective rationality of the universe as the ground of genuine knowledge, and of reconnecting theological and scientific concepts that had fallen apart under the stress of Augustinian dualism, but it also had the effect of injecting into Western thought concepts of a damaging kind, not least those bound up with a fundamental change in the doctrine of God. Here Christian theology had a bad and not just a good influence on the development of science. It took up certain patristic ideas of the immutability of God—already influenced by Jewish and Hellenic thought—and of the impassibility of God, the idea that God does not suffer change or hurt or pain. In taking up these ideas, it changed them by correlating them with the notion of God as the Unmoved Mover, which gave rise to a static concept of God. The difficulty presented by this new concept of God is this: if God is immutable and impassible, he remains utterly detached from the universe and constitutes what in science we call an "inertial system." That is to say, he is a God who affects the universe without interacting with it; he affects it inertially by what Aristotle called "the activity of immobility," for no actual motion passes from God as Mover to what he "moves." The counterpart to this concept of God is a universe of necessity, i.e., a reinterpretation of the pervading rationality of nature as a system of logico-causal connections inertially imposed upon the universe by a detached and immutable God.

The upshot of this was the *loss of contingence*. The Greek way of thinking, now reintroduced into Christian culture, has great difficulty in taking contingence seriously as a rational concept, for it identifies rationality with necessity. It can think contingence rationally—up to a point at any rate—only if there is an element of necessity in it, but this means that to think contingence is to think it away in order to think the element of necessity in it. That is why medieval theology and science could not hold on to the radical doctrine of contingence, let alone contingent intelligibility, developed by classical Christian theology. There is not a little discussion in medieval literature about *contingentia*, especially in relation to the question of whether God can foresee contingent events, and therefore to the question of the freedom of the world in relation to God. It is ultimately a determinist view that prevails—which, admittedly, through its teleological slant opens out a little the conception of a closed causal system, but at the same time allows the universal application of the Aristotelian notion of causality in intramundane relations.

Now the doctrine of the immutability and impassibility of God as we find it in patristic theology is ambiguous. It means that God is not moved by, and is not changed by, anything outside himself, and that he is not affected by anything or does not suffer from anything beyond himself. In this sense the immutability and impassibility of God refer to the eternal tranquility and serenity of God in his transcendence over all the changes and chances, all the pain and violence, of our world. But it does not mean that God does not move himself and is incapable of imparting motion to what he has made. It does not mean that God in himself is devoid of passion, devoid of love, or devoid of mercy, that he is impassibly and immutably related to our world of space and time in such a way that it is thrown back upon itself as a closed continuum of cause and effect. I grant that patristic theology was tempted constantly by the thrust of Greek thought to change the concepts of impassibility and immutability in this direction, but it remained entrenched within the orbit of the Judeo-Christian doctrine of the living God who moves himself, who through his free love created the universe, imparting to its dynamic order, and who through the outgoing of his love moves outside of himself in the incarnation.

Let us pause for a moment to consider what this means, something which Greek patristic thought wrestled with through Athanasius and later on through John of Damascus: God was not eternally Creator. Athanasius rejected the idea that God is eternally Creator and its attendant idea that the creation eternally exists in the mind of God, for the creation of the world out of nothing meant that it had an absolute beginning. That implies, staggeringly, that even in the life of God there is change: God was not eternally Creator; he became Creator in the free act of creation. Nor was God eternally incarnate, for in Jesus Christ he became what he never was eternally, a creature, without of course ceasing to be the eternal God. In the incarnation, therefore, something new happened, even for God, when, out of his free, outgoing love, he moved outside of himself, and in the incarnation of his Son, he forever bound himself up indissolubly with our creaturely being— such was the staggering extent of his love for the world. Here then we have no static conception of God, but in greater force than ever, a doctrine of the living, acting God who is in himself a fullness of love and indeed an infinite communion of love who freely pours himself out on the universe he has made, giving it through the incarnation to share in the love that God is in the depths of his own Being; not a doctrine, therefore, of a God who is inertially, impassibly, or passively related to our world, but on the contrary a doctrine of God who, in the living movement of the love which he is precisely as God, interacts with our creaturely world.

That is the teaching that altered the whole concept of God, of his Being and his Act, in the early centuries of our era. Its revolutionary implications were clearly brought out by Athanasius when he showed that, since the Act and Word of God we meet in Jesus Christ are eternally inherent in the Being of God, and since none other than the very Being of God himself is mediated to us through the incarnation of his love in Act and Word in Jesus Christ, God's Being is revealed to be his Being in his Act and Word— Being that is intrinsically dynamic and eloquent, the Being of the ever living, acting, and loving God. That is the basic doctrine of God that in our day has been resurrected out of patristic theology and given massive exposition in modern idiom by Karl Barth in his account of the Being of God in his Act, and of the Act of God in his Being, inseparably bound up with the transcendent freedom of God in his love. Such a doctrine of God, wherever it is found, demands a rather different notion of the universe than that which arose out of the medieval world with its covert Deism and determinism—but that is to anticipate.

We return to the point that medieval theology reinforced and developed the concept of the unity and objective rationality of the universe, but in such a way that it really lost the concepts of contingence and freedom and was rather blind to the all-important concept of contingent intelligibility. We must now ask how the masterful ideas of unitary rationality, contingent intelligibility, and contingent freedom fared in the scientific revolution of the sixteenth and seventeenth centuries, when there took place the great switch from static to dynamic concepts that characterized the change from the old to the new world.

Here without doubt we must take our cue from Isaac

Newton, for it was he who supplied the basic paradigms within which modern science has operated until the early years of our century. Newton accepted fully the idea of the rationality and stability of the universe as grounded in the rationality and stability of God—although his concept of God was much closer to the medieval than to the patristic view. In order to explain that he developed the grand conception, to which I have already alluded, of absolute, mathematical time and space and relative, apparent time and space. While the latter refers to the phenomenal world—the world relative to the human observer and therefore variable—the former refers to the fixed frame of reference in terms of which we seek to understand the world irrespective of the observer. But this fixed frame of reference—absolute, mathematical time and space—Newton identified with the mind of God, which contains and imposes objective order upon the universe. God contains the universe, however, without being affected by it impassibly and immutably—that is what Newton meant by the term *absolute* in this connection. But if God inertially contains and regulates the universe without being affected by it, there is no interaction between God and the universe in the biblical or patristic sense—that is why Newton found himself having to reject the incarnation, and even to support Arius against Athanasius! Newton's God was so transcendentally related to the universe that he was deistically detached from it through his immutability and impassibility. It was, then, on this deeply dualist basis that Newton developed his grand synthesis of God and the universe that allowed him to explain the immutable, eternal laws of nature as they are grounded objectively in the immutability and eternity of God. This differed from the medieval understanding of nature as a causally ordered system, in that it operated with a Galilean and not an Aristotelian concept of motion, and described the universe as a system of bodies in motion reduced to orderly understanding through mathematical or mechanical principles, which in the nature of the case ruled out "final causes" in the Aristotelian sense. Thus we have the rise of the mechanistic conception of the universe.

A difficult ambiguity developed in Newton's own position in respect to the relation of the universe to God. On the one hand, he held that while the universe is to be explained throughout in causal or mechanical terms, the universe itself as a whole cannot be explained in this way, because of the kind of connection that obtains within it. A connection of a different kind is required to account for the origin of the universe or for its initial conditions, i.e., in its relation with God. However it is to be explained, this correlation of the universe with God implied that it is finally an open system. This was very important for Newton, for it meant that the universe is not to be regarded as closed in upon itself, a consistent and complete system in itself, a system that is not finally self-explanatory. As a rational system the universe is only intelligible if there is a sufficient reason for it beyond itself—in God. On the other hand, Newton held that there were certain irregularities in the planetary and stellar system that could not be explained in terms of his laws of motion alone, which seemed to require the regulative control of God. Hence, Newton felt constrained to bring God within the system of efficient causes as an explanatory factor to account for the alleged gaps in nature, to preserve the harmony of the universe, and to prevent irregularities.

This gave rise to considerable confusion in the history of thought. As Newtonian science developed, the so-called irregularities disappeared before further experimental evidence and the rigorous extension of the laws of motion, until eventually Laplace argued that there was no need for that hypothesis "God," for he claimed to be able to explain the systematic order of the universe entirely in terms of self-regulating principles and the internal stability of the universe. This yielded a concept of the mechanistic universe as entirely closed in upon itself, with a tightly drawn determinism. Certainly the Newtonians were right in rejecting the second role Newton attributed to God in the universe—as an explanatory and regulative principle within the system of efficient causes—but that did not by any means destroy Newton's primary point that the universe as a whole is not explainable in terms of the kind of order that obtains within it, and that it cannot therefore be conceived as a mechanical system complete and consistent in itself. In other words, Newton insisted that the universe is ultimately a contingent system, which as such requires a sufficient reason for its rationality beyond itself. Here the advance of scientific thought has proved Newton right and Laplace wrong. This is apparent, for example, in the regular collapse of so-called "steady state" or "oscillating" views of the universe before the sheer singularity of the universe. But it also receives justification from the application of the famous Gödelian theorems, which demonstrate that any logico-deductive system of arthmetic or logic of sufficient richness is consistent only if it is incomplete in itself, or, if it is consistent, it is so only through reference to a level of rational connections beyond it—theorems that apply to mechanical as well as mathematical and logical systems.

That is what we now realize, but in the history of thought it was otherwise. When Newton's second role for God was found to be unnecessary, many people dropped from their thought the first role Newton attributed to God as well, and so tended to become agnostics or atheists. When Newton's first role for God was dropped, however, the conception of the contingence of the universe tended to go with it, which was an immense obstruction to the advance of modern science. By and large the Newtonian outlook, with its conception of a mechanistic universe correlated to an immutable and impassible Deity, gave rise to a massive deism that, if it did not always dominate, certainly lay menacingly in the background of Western and especially Protestant thought. That is the context in which much "modern theology" still operates; and that is the ground on which "demythologizing" arises. With the axiomatic assumption of a deistic disjunction between God and the world, where living interaction between God and the world is ruled out, miracles are denigrated as supernatural interference in our world or as infringements of the laws of nature, and of course the incarnation has to be explained away in some symbolic way—but all these ideas go back to the hard dualism of the Newtonian outlook, and they stand or fall with it.

At this point it must be added that while Newton's own thought powerfully established in his way the concept of the objective rationality of the universe, the dualism with which he operated between the mathematical and the apparent gave rise with the Kantians and the positivists to such a phenomenological abstraction of appearances from their geometric foundations that the concept of objective rationality suffered severely, frequently to be replaced by the notion of "regulative principles" deriving from the structure of the mind or arising from regular scientific conventions. Hence, until fairly recently the concept of objective rationality has been pushed out of the way, and in the Kantian revival of necessitarianism and determinism, the notions of contingent intelligibility and contingent freedom went with it. Paradoxically, however, the increasing emphasis upon experimental science could not help but keep the idea of contingence alive, if only because it relied upon it in practice, even when it is found rejected in the pronouncements of scientists!

Today everything has changed, and changed drastically, for with the work of Planck and Einstein science took an irreversible turn in another direction, away from Ptolemaic and Newtonian dualisms, and established for itself epistemological foundations in a profound ontological and dynamic integration of theoretical and empirical ingredients in human knowledge, and thus restored to its proper place the concept of a rationality objectively inherent in the universe independent of our perceiving and conceiving of it. What is more, the ideas of contingent intelligibility and contingent freedom have been forced through sheer scientific rigor to break cover and come to the front after having been submerged for so long by necessitarian and determinist views of nature. That is to say, science itself has found that the more deeply it penetrated into the structures of the created universe, the more it has had to operate with the very basic ideas that classical Christian theology produced in the early centuries of our era. Thus, with the end of determinism, and the discovery that the universe is, not a closed, but an open or nonequilibrium system, a genuine contingency is massively restored. In its macroscopic and its microscopic aspects alike, the universe confronts us with possibilities of disclosing itself in ways that our science cannot anticipate. It possesses a spontaneity and a way of surprising us in its contingent freedom that we cannot bring under the control of any necessities in our arguments or technologies. Thus there is revealed to be intrinsic in the universe, a contingent intelligibility of such an indefinite range in objectivity that it stretches far beyond the frontiers and limits of human science. Thus we are back at such an outlook upon the universe as Christian theology reaches when on the double ground of the creation and incarnation it finds that through the free, outgoing love of God this universe is correlated to the unlimited rationality, freedom, and spontaneity of the Creator.

What am I saying here? Not that theology today must be grounded upon the new science, but rather that this science, in point of fact, rests upon foundational ideas that science did not and could not have produced on its own, ideas that derive from the Christian understanding of the relation of God to the universe. Under the grace of God there has arisen in the history of civilization a science that has a liberating effect upon nature, delivering it from the artificial abstractions of our human invention and imposition, but delivering us also from imprisonment in these abstractions. The new science has thus been peeling away pseudo-concepts with which theology has so long been suffocated and to which, alas, it has so often submitted and betrayed itself. Thus the effect of the new science upon theology is to help it to be truer to its own foundations, the foundations that were laid when Christian thought struggled with the dualist modes of thought entrenched in Greek culture and produced the revolutionary ideas of unitary rationality, contingent intelligibility, and contingent freedom.

What, then, is the task of Christian theology today? It must be the same as that of Christian theology in the early centuries when it undertook this reconstruction of the bases of Greek culture as part of the evangelizing activity of the Church, with the hope that Christianity would take root in a developing Christian culture. Today we live in a world being changed by science, which is far more congenial to Christian theology than any period in the history of Western civilization. Here the task of Christian theology must be the recovery of the doctrines of creation and incarnation in such a way that we think through their interrelations more rigorously than ever before, and on that ground engage in constant dialogue with the new science, which can only be to the benefit of both.

4

The Transformation of

Natural Theology

IN THE PREVIOUS LECTURE I sought to show that Christian theology and natural science operate with certain basic ideas, without which neither would be what it is, revealing that there is a deep interrelation between theology and science. These ideas arose in connection with the fact that since theology has to do not simply with God/man relations but with God/man/world or God/world/man relations, an understanding of the world inevitably enters into the coefficients of theological concepts and statements. Moreover, they were derived through theological reflection on the relation of the incarnation to the creation, and thus had a distinctively Christian source. They are not ideas that natural science, let alone Greek science, could ever have produced on its own, but they have proved themselves utterly essential to our empirico-theoretical scientific enterprise and advance in knowledge. The role of these ideas has

[75]

never, in fact, been so evident or powerful as it is today. If there is this deep natural connection between theology and science, such that they share basic ideas that are natural to science and natural to theology, that common basis must surely be the proper ground for a natural theology. But if these basic ideas have a definitely Christian source, and are grounded ultimately on divine revelation, in what sense may we speak here of a "natural theology"?

In the history of thought, what is known traditionally as "natural theology" came to the fore and flourished during periods in which dualist modes of thought prevailed in science and philosophy and in which knowledge was allegedly derived by way of abstraction from sense-experience or deduction from observations. This was particularly the case in the Middle Ages, when the great natural theology of the Schoolmen flourished, and in the so-called Age of Reason, when, especially after Newton and Locke, natural theology was brought back from its depreciation in the Reformation and was put to service by English deism. Sometimes justification for this traditional type of natural theology is sought by tracing it back to writings of early Christian theologians addressed to unbelievers outside the Church, such as the *Contra Gentes* of Athanasius, in which he showed that as we let our minds tune in to the rational order that pervades the universe, they are already on the way that leads to the really existent God. No attempt was made there to find a way of reaching God by logical reasoning, but rather to point out a way of communing with the regulative and providential activity of God in the rational order of the universe, in which our minds come under the force of the truth of God as it bears upon us in its own self-evidence and shines through to us in its own light. This order pervading the universe does not derive from some immanent cosmological reason, or *logos*, such as the philosophers envisage, but from the uncreated and creative *Logos* of God, in whose image, by the grace of God, we ourselves have been created, so that as we contemplate the rational order in the creation, we are directed above and beyond ourselves to the one God, the Lord of creation. The *Contra Gentes*, however, is a twin to another treatise, the *De Incarnatione*, in which we are directed to the incarnation of the *Logos* who gave the creation its order, but who has condescended to become man within the structures of the creation and to reveal himself intimately and redemptively to us—for it is in and through this relation to the *Logos* in his incarnate reality that we may be liberated from all that is irrational and disorderly to apprehend in an appropriate and worthy manner the loving and rational activity of God in creation and salvation. Thus the *Contra Gentes* and the *De Incarnatione* together show how, through heuristic inquiry within the field of God/man/world or God/world/man interconnections, we may find a way into the central unity or order of things that is then allowed to throw light upon the whole manifold of connections with which we are concerned in the knowledge of God in his interaction with the creation—and not least the distinctive kind of intelligible relation appropriate to its actual subject-matter. It is within the compass of that integrated theological understanding of creation and incarnation that we have embedded the argumentation that some would regard as "natural theology." However, what Athanasius is doing there is to show that knowledge of God and knowledge of the world share the same ultimate foundations in the *Logos*, or Rationality, of God the Creator. He does not operate with any distinction between natural or supernatural knowledge. Hence, what he has to say there of the knowledge of the world in its intrinsic intelligibility and order, within which God is known, cannot be abstracted and made to stand on its own, for it holds good and is consistent only in a deep and unbreakable polarity with our actual knowledge of God revealed in and through Jesus Christ.

This integrated theological understanding of God and the world, however, becomes rather ambiguous in the thought of John of Damascus in the eighth century, that is, once the Neoplatonic-Byzantine dualism has set in and a gap is opened up between the unknowable, unnameable God and the conceptual categories with which we operate. This gap is most evident in the writings of the Pseudo-Dionysius, in which we find a supertranscendental approach to God that relativizes and devaluates even the concept of God as Father. Something had to be done to close this dangerous chasm in Byzantine theology, and so we find John of Damascus introducing into it ideas with which Athanasius would have nothing to do, such as the Aristotelian notions of space and motion and of the Unmoved Mover. Presumably he thought they would be helpful, but actually they only served to harden the latent dualism. In this context we find something like a natural theology in the later sense, claiming demonstrative proof, and there is a strange confusion between theology and cosmology in the account of the relation of God to the structures within the created cosmos. Nevertheless, in the thought of John of Damascus this kind of natural theology is not divided from the rest of his theology, for it is not finally abstracted from the activity of God in revelation and redemption. There are deep ambiguities in it, however, nowhere more evident than in the uneasy juxtaposition of his doctrine of the Trinity, which he plagiarized from Pseudo-Cyril, and of his Neoplatonic idea of God—who is so incomprehensible and nameless that we can know him only indirectly through things related to him. Internal inconsistency is inevitable, for example, in an understanding of the universe as created out of nothing, yet as timelessly held in God's thoughts, which are the predetermination, image, and pattern of its determinate existence—which reminds us of the ambiguity in this respect to be found in the thought of St. Thomas Aquinas, deriving from his juxtaposition of natural theology and revealed theology.

It was in fact on the foundations laid by John of Damascus that Western thinkers like St. Thomas based their natural theology, but in his case we have an explicit division between natural and supernatural knowledge, which is rooted in the Augustinian-Aristotelian dualism in his thought. This relation of the division between natural and revealed theology to dualist thought of this kind is highly significant, for it points to a double impact upon it from the underlying cosmological and epistemological dualisms. On the one hand, there is involved here a deep (but usually covert) deistic disjunction between God and the world, with a stress upon the transcendence of God that carried with it no idea of an active relation between God and the world. God "moves" or "acts" only in the sense of arousing action already latent in the world. Theologically, this necessitated within the Augustinian tradition some intermediate realm of "grace" as constituting the practical or effective relation between God and nature or God and man. This implied an intimate relation between nature and grace that affected the meaning of the term *natural* in "natural theology." On the other hand, there is at work here a split within intramundane experience between signs and things signified, giving rise to the notion of "significates" between signs and realities signified, which came to be invested with an ontological status and thus gave rise to false ontologies; but also a split between thought and being, or idea and event, necessitating an intermediary realm of representations, images or ideas "in the middle," as they were called—the sense-data of later times. Within Aristotelian phenomenalism this meant that we operate with ideas that are derived by abstraction from sense-experience, but if this posited a logical bridge between concepts and experience in their discovery, it had also to operate with a logical bridge between concepts and experience in their verification. Within the context of this cosmological and epistemological dualism, it was inevitable that a natural theology should be thrown up, the primary task of which was to close the gap between the world and God by means of a logical bridge, and that is what in their combined way the famous "Five Ways," by which natural knowledge of God was claimed to be demonstrated, sought to do. The logicist nature of this enterprise is particularly evident when attempts were mistakenly made to recast St. Anselm's "ontological argument" into a logical form, making it dependent on a logico-necessary relation between our idea of God and his Reality, which was bound to fail but which reveals the weakness of the whole enterprise in that form. The strongest of the arguments developed by medieval natural theology was the cosmological argument which depends on the contingency of the universe, but that argument could not be consistently maintained within an epistemological outlook in which the rational was identified with the necessary—which Leibniz was not slow to point out as he recast the cosmological argument in a more acceptable form.

Much the same kind of natural theology arose when after the Reformation the Augustinian-Aristotelian dualism was replaced by one that can be characterized as Augustinian-Newtonian. Meantime there had taken place the great transition from a medieval to a modern conception of science, which meant that natural theology could only be developed in the modern world on the ground of our knowledge of the world and of nature achieved by natural science. But here again the derivation of ideas was explained in terms of abstraction from sense-experience or of logical deduction from observations, with all the attendant problems of what was called "representative perception," or the intermediary realm of sense-data between the mind and reality. Thus, a deep epistemological split opened up between the theoretical and the empirical, between form and being, or as Heidegger expressed it, there took place a damaging secession of *logos* from being, leading to a logical tyranny of abstract ideas over being. It was within this context of rising positivism in philosophy and science, with its doctrine of a logical bridge between concepts and experience, that the new natural theology renewed the attempt to throw a logical bridge between our knowledge and experience of this world and knowledge of God, for if there is a logical bridge—as positivist phenomenalism and deductivism claimed—between experience and concepts in the discovery of ideas, it must also be possible to operate with a logical bridge between concepts and experience in the verification of those ideas. Such a natural theology was bound to collapse as soon as this positivist position was finally undermined, and that is what happened—partly through the increasing rigor of logical analysis in the alignment of logic and mathematics, in which positivism, as it were, "predicted" its own downfall, but above all through a rigorous scientific rejection of dualism and the realization that in the indissoluble interpenetration of theoretical and empirical elements in our experiences and cognitions, there is no merely logical way to the discovery and establishment of new knowledge.

Before we proceed further, however, it will be instructive to note the differences between medieval and post-Newtonian natural theology. Medieval natural theology was powerfully slanted by its background in Greek science and the Ptolemaic cosmology, in which the fundamental orientation of thought was away from what is transient and particular or singular to what is eternal and universal. This passage of thought took place through a sort of reduction upwards of accidental or contingent phenomena and events to a realm of necessary forms and unchanging essences, which inevitably inhibited empirical inquiry and knowledge. In line with this also was the distinctive medieval understanding of the world—in which full force was given to final causes in the Aristotelian sense, so that everything in the world was construed through an ultimate teleological relation to God. But since nature was regarded as impregnated with final causes in this way, natural theologians imagined they could read the eternal patterns off the book of nature, which often led in practice to substituting nature for God, but also contributed heavily to the sacralization of the universe so distinctive in medieval culture and art. The great strength of medieval theology was two-fold. On the one hand, it lay in the acceptance and development of the conception of the objective rationality of the universe as grounded in the rationality of God, and on the other hand, it lay in the otherworldly orientation of mind that discerned meaning in the universe as a whole in its semantic and sacramental reference beyond the temporal and the visible to the eternal and the invisible realm of God. Both of these aspects of thought helped to undergird the weaknesses in the logical argumentations of natural theology and thus gave it a strength that cannot be detected by logical analysis. But when we add to this the prevalent concept of "Augustinian" grace intimately relating nature to God, the question must be asked, as, for example, of St. Thomas, whether his natural theology was altogether what it appeared to be—for even he admitted that the reason with which natural theology operates is reason that has already been baptized and through divine grace has been adapted to God.

Post-Newtonian natural theology was also heavily slanted by its background in science and cosmology as they had been transformed through the work of Copernicus, Galileo, and Newton. In contrast to the essentialist science of the medieval world, this science was directed to the world of observable, contingent phenomena, which it regarded as accessible to empirical and rational inquiry, without reference to abstract essences. It was concerned with the concrete and the particular as well as the general, with bodies in motion and all the manifestations of nature, which it attempted to explain in terms of quantifiable connections, that is, through the application of mathematical coordinates and equations, without the introduction of final causes, yet in such a way that knowledge of the world could be harnessed for the advance of man's place within the world. Here we have a movement of thought away from the other world to this world, in a reduction downward in a physicalist direction from phenomena to atomic particles and their external connections, that yielded a mechanistic and materialist outlook. Behind this orientation there lay also the powerful Reformation emphasis upon the creation of the universe out of nothing that broke the stranglehold of necessary and changeless forms in the medieval understanding of the world, liberating the concept of the contingence of the world which demanded that it had to be investigated through empirical questioning of its own latent processes and patterns. The situation, however, was highly ambiguous. This is nowhere more evident than in the thought of Newton himself, who on the one hand accepted the fact that, as created out of nothing, the universe is contingent upon the will of God and his government over it as the Almighty Lord of Creation, but on the other hand insisted that the universe is contained by the immensity and infinity of God, who, regarded as immutable and impassible, constituted an inertial system in reference to which a causal interpretation of the universe of bodies in motion could only turn out to be determinist. In this context Protestant natural theology was fraught with great ambiguities, but its strength lay, on the one hand, in the acceptance of the unitary rationality of the universe (and indeed until Kant in its objective rationality), and on the other hand, in its understanding of the contingency of the universe that could have ultimate meaning only if the intelligible relations within the universe, in terms of which it was scientifically interpreted, were grounded in a sufficient reason beyond it in God. Thus, once again it is the cosmological argument developed by natural theology that proves to be the most powerful.

THE TRANSFORMATION OF NATURAL THEOLOGY

At the same time, in spite of the great revival of Augustinian theology in the Churches of the Reformation, the weakness of Protestant natural theology lay in the increasing secularization of culture, grounded, paradoxically, in the doctrine of creation out of nothing, which meant that, if we are to understand the world in its contingent processes, we must examine them in such a way that we turn our back upon God, as it were—*acsi deus non daretur*, as Grotius said so pointedly—for God as such does not enter into the system of efficient causes and cannot be included, therefore, within the coefficients of mathematico-causal explanations of those processes. Hence, after the place given to God in Newton's system of the world was dropped from scientific thought, scientific concentration upon understanding the universe out of itself had the effect of shutting it up within itself, with consequent widespread loss of meaning in any semantic reference beyond the world. Thus a secularization of culture set in, in sharp contrast to the sacralization of culture in the medieval outlook. Moreover, with the elimination of final causes and all the immanent teleology that involved in our understanding of nature, the deistic breach between God and the world he had made became rather wider in Protestant than in Roman natural theology, which made it all the more imperative for natural theology, if it was to exist at all, to throw a logical bridge across the gap to God—but that is the very point where it suffered such a denouement.

I do not propose to discuss the history of thought that led up to the collapse of natural theology in its traditional form, medieval (including neo-Thomist) and post-Newtonian. It will be sufficient to indicate several lines of attack to which natural theology was laid open: Humean skepticism about the nature and validity of causal connection and the error of confounding relations of matters of fact and relations of ideas; Kantian critique of the possibility of natural theology within the limits of pure reason, together with the rejection of objective intelligibility in knowledge and the cutting of any cognitive link between faith and God; the positivist radicalization of Humean and Kantian criticism that emanated from the "Vienna Circle," together with the rejection of all metaphysical claims of a relation between thought and being as "meaningless," which applies, of course, no less to science than it does to religion. The effect of this developing criticism was to suggest that a natural theology might be built up in such a way that logical argumentation was replaced by moral argument (an idea that stems from Kant himself), or might be replaced by some form of a phenomenological and existentialist argument arising out of man's self-understanding as he seeks an explanation for his existence within the universe (which is found particularly among Roman Catholic thinkers). None of these new approaches really touches the root of the problem, however, which lies in the epistemological and cosmological dualisms that gave rise to the traditional form of natural theology in the first place, and to the attendant intramundane splits in human culture and knowledge that have affected the form natural theology has taken within the Augustinian-Newtonian, as well as the Augustinian-Aristotelian, outlooks. If natural theology is to have a viable reconstruction even in something like its traditional form, it can be only on the basis of a restored ontology in which our thought operates with a fundamental unity of concept and experience, or of form and being, within a contingent but inherently intelligible and open-structured universe. That is the kind of natural theology, in the context of our modern scientific outlook, of which E. L. Mascall has given such a powerful account in his Edinburgh Gifford Lectures of 1971 entitled *The Openness of Being: Natural Theology Today*.

How are we, in the light of all this, to understand Karl Barth's objections to natural theology? They certainly have nothing at all to do with some kind of deistic dualism between God and the world implying no active relation between God and the world, or with some form of Marcionite dualism between redemption and creation implying a depreciation of the creature, as so many of Barth's critics have averred; nor have they to do with a skepticism coupled with a false fideism, such as was condemned by the First Vatican Council. On the contrary, Barth's position rests upon an immense stress on the concrete activity of God in space and time, in creation as in redemption, and upon his refusal to accept that God's power is limited by the weakness of human capacity or that the so-called natural reason can set any limits to God's self-revelation to mankind. The failure to understand Barth at this point is highly revealing, for it indicates that his critics themselves still think within the dualist modes of thought that Barth had himself long left behind, in his restoration of an interactionist understanding of the relation between God and the world in which he operated with an ontological and cognitive bridge between the world and God, which God himself has already established. Thus Barth's objections to traditional natural theology are on grounds precisely the opposite of those attributed to him!

Barth's thought, it must be understood, moves within the orbit of the Reformation's restored emphasis on the creation of the world out of nothing and thus upon its utter contingence, in which the natural is once again allowed to be natural, for nature is set free from the hidden divinization imposed upon it when it was considered to be impregnated with final causes—the notion of *deus sive natura*. That is the way nature is treated if God is actually thought of as deistically detached from it, so that nature can in some measure substitute for God by providing out of itself a bridge to the divine. Hence Barth attacked the kind of Augustinian metaphysics advocated by Erich Przywara, in which the Aristotelian notion of a divine entelechy embedded in nature was reinforced with a Neoplatonic notion of infused grace and enlightenment. Thus it could be claimed that all being is intrinsically analogical to the divine and that man endowed with grace is inherently capable of participating in God. Barth understood the immanentism latent in this theology to be the other side of the deism he found so unacceptable, and in contrast he emphasized all the more the Godness of God and the humanity of man, substituting for an illicit divinity inherent in man—which could easily be made the ground for a synthesis between God and the world—the Judeo-Christian understanding of God's creative, revelatory, and redemptive activity in space and time, as it had come to formulated expression in the theology of the Early Church, when Christians thought out the interrelation between the incarnation and the creation.

Barth's particularly sharp opposition to Przywara's thought was due to his conviction that this was, from the Roman Catholic side, a new version of the immanentist philosophy that lay behind German romantic idealist thought, within the thought-forms of which Protestant theology in Germany had been so imprisoned that it had lost the ground for any effective opposition to the demonic natural theology of the Nazis. This was also the reason for his no-less-sharp rejection of Emil Brunner's attempt to provide a basis for a Protestant natural theology on the double ground of nature and grace, without coming to grips with the fundamental issues at stake. Apart from these polemics, however, Barth's real objection to traditional natural theology rested on theological and scientific grounds. It is the actual content of our knowledge of God, together with the scientific method that inheres in it, that excludes any movement of thought that arises on some other, independent ground as ultimately irrelevant and as an inevitable source of confusion when it is adduced as a second or coordinate basis for positive theology.

So far as theological content is concerned, Barth's argument runs like this. If the God whom we have actually come to know through Jesus Christ really *is* Father, Son, and Holy Spirit in his own eternal and undivided Being, then what are we to make of an independent natural theology that terminates, not upon the Being of the Triune God—i.e., upon God as he really is in himself—but upon some Being of God in general? Natural theology by its very operation abstracts the existence of God from his act, so that if it does not begin with deism, it imposes deism upon theology. If really to know God through his saving activity in our world is to know him as Triune, then the doctrine of the Trinity belongs to the very groundwork of knowledge of God from the very start, which calls in question any doctrine of God as the One God gained apart from his trinitarian activity—but that is the kind of knowledge of God that is yielded in natural theology of the traditional kind.

So far as scientific method is concerned, Barth demands a rigorous mode of inquiry in which form and content, method and subject-matter are inseparably joined together, and he rejects any notion that we can establish how we know apart from our actual knowledge and its material content. Thus Barth stands squarely on the same grounds as rigorous science when he insists on the freedom to develop a scientific method appropriate to the field of theological inquiry and to elaborate epistemological structures under the compulsion of the nature of the object as it becomes disclosed in the progress of the inquiry, quite untrammelled by *a priori* assumptions of any kind or by any preconceptions deriving from some other field of investigation. As an *a posteriori* science, theology involves the questioning of all presuppositions and all structures of thought independent of or antecedent to its own operations. This is why Barth makes so much of the epistemological implications of justification by grace alone, for it forces upon us relentless questioning of all we thought we knew beforehand, or of all prejudgments and external authorities, philosophical or ecclesiastical, in such a way that in the last resort theology is thrown back wholly upon the nature and activity of God for the justification or verification of our concepts and statements about him. It is here in the doctrine of justification that we can see clearly how form and content, method and subject-matter, in theological inquiry coincide.

Epistemologically, then, what Barth objects to in traditional natural theology is not any invalidity in its argumentation, nor even its rational structure, as such, but its *independent* character—i.e., the autonomous rational structure that natural theology develops on the ground of "nature alone," in abstraction from the active self-disclosure of the living and Triune God—for that can only split the knowledge of God into two parts, natural knowledge of the One God and revealed knowledge of the Triune God, which is scientifically as well as theologically intolerable. This is not to reject the place of a proper rational structure in knowledge of God, such as natural theology strives for, but to insist that unless that rational structure is intrinsically bound up with the actual content of knowledge of God, it is a distorting abstraction. That is why Barth claims that, properly understood, natural theology is included *within* revealed theology, where we have to do with actual knowledge of God as it is grounded in the intelligible relations in God himself, for it is there under the compulsion of God's self-disclosure in Being and Act that the rational structure appropriate to him arises in our understanding of him. But in the nature of the case it is not a rational structure that can be abstracted from the actual knowledge of God with which it is integrated, and made to stand on its own as an independent or autonomous system of thought, for then it would be meaningless, like something that is complete and consistent in itself but without any ontological reference beyond itself: it becomes merely a game to be enjoyed like chess—which Barth is as ready to enjoy as much as anyone else, although he cannot take it seriously.

In order to explain and develop Barth's position here, let me borrow an analogy from Einstein's essay "Geometry and Experience." The rise of four-dimensional geometries of space and time has revealed to us that Euclidean geometry is an idealization, a distorting abstraction of geometry from experience or from empirical reality, in which it has been erected into a self-contained conceptual system on its own, pursued as a purely theoretic science antecedent to physics, in which we develop our actual knowledge of the world. Thus it is evident that physics, as we now pursue it within the spatio-temporal structures of the real world, cannot be subjected to the framework of Euclidean geometry without radical distortion and loss of its essential dynamic and material content. Rather must geometry be put into the heart of physics, where it is pursued in indissoluble unity with physics as the sub-science of its inner rational or epistemological structure and as an essential part of its empirico-theoretical grasp of reality in its objective intelligible relations. As such, however, the character of geometry changes, for it takes on the character of a natural science, that is, a science natural to the space-time structures of the real world. There it remains geometry—but not as a conceptual system complete in itself, for it is consistent as geometry only as it is completed beyond itself in the material content of physics. As geometry in the heart of physics, it is open to logical analysis and description, but it becomes empty and useless, so far as actual knowledge is concerned, so soon as it is torn out of its natural bed in physics and erected into a conceptual system on its own.

On that analogy, we can understand Karl Barth's rejection of an *independent* natural theology—treated as a conceptual system on its own, antecedent to the rise and formulation of actual knowledge of God. Rather must it be brought within the body of positive theology, where it is integrated with its material content and pursued in indissoluble unity with it. But now the whole character of natural theology becomes transformed, for pursued within the actual inquiry of scientific theology, where we must think rigorously in accordance with the self-disclosure of God in his own intelligible relations, it will become *natural* to the material content of theology and will fall under the determination of its inherent intelligibility. No longer extrinsic but intrinsic to actual knowledge of God, it will function as the essential sub-structure within theological science, in which we are concerned to develop the inner material logic that arises in our inquiry and understanding of God. As natural geometry is the space-time structure embedded in a dynamic and realist physics, so natural theology is the space-time structure embedded in a dynamic and realist theology. Looked at in this light Barth's exclusion of an independent natural theology assumes a formidable character, for surely no genuinely scientific inquiry can let itself be controlled by an independent logical structure, even by conceding to it any claims to constitute an indispensable precondition or a prior understanding for the inquiry in question.

It seems evident, then, that Barth's opposition to the traditional type of natural theology, which is pursued as an independent system on its own, antecedent to positive or revealed theology, rests upon a radical rejection of its dualist basis and constitutes a return to the kind of unitary thinking we find in classical Christian theology as exemplified by Athanasius, in which theology is committed to one coherent framework of thought that arises within the unitary interaction of God with our world in creation and incarnation, and in which we are unable to make any separation between a natural and a supernatural knowledge of God. This account of Barth's thought in relation to natural theology is not meant to imply that Barth was always consistent himself, but it is meant to show the main lines of the position he developed—which, as far as I can see, is one that on its own terms and on its own ground is basically consistent with the positions we adopt today in natural science. But if Barth's position is to be accepted, as I believe it is, then I also believe that there must be a deeper connection between the basic concepts of theological science and natural science than he seemed to allow: or, otherwise expressed, there is a *natural* connection between theological science and natural science. If that is the case, then a proper natural theology should be *natural* both to theological science and to natural science. A natural theology in this full sense will have its proper place in the dialogue between theological science and natural science within their common sharing of the rational structures of space and time conferred on the universe by God in his creating of it, and within their common sharing in the basic conceptions of the unitary rationality of the universe, its contingent intelligibility and contingent freedom—which derive, as we have seen, from a Christian understanding of the relation of God to the universe. Insofar as natural theology is indissolubly bound up with the inner rational and epistemological structure of our inquiry into the relation of God to the universe, what it is may become clearer when these lectures are completed, for they all bear upon this question.

Meantime, however, for the remainder of this lecture, let us consider a little the bearing of the unity of form and being upon the main point in the traditional ontological argument and the bearing of the singularity of the universe, as it is thrust upon us again by modern cosmology, upon the main point in the traditional cosmological argument. In neither case will we be concerned with independent argumentation, but with an examination of the epistemological structure of knowledge of God in his relation to us in the world in these respects, that is, within the unitary movement of theological understanding. Inevitably, in the focus of attention upon the unity of form and being and the singularity of the universe, some measure of temporary, methodological "bracketing" of these issues will be entailed— but solely in the recognition that what we thus consider is complete only in the integrated unity of Christian theology, and fulfills its role there within the stratified structure of knowledge of God (which we shall consider later) on its proper level of connection in coordination with the other levels.

(a) *The unity of form and being.* Our problem here is that for many, many centuries Western thought has suffered from such a disruption of the unity of form and being, due to underlying dualisms and the abstractive processes in thought to which they give rise, that the detachment of form from being has become almost second nature to us. Hence, the kind of readjustment demanded of us by the revolution in scientific knowledge, evident, for example, in relativity theory, is not easy to make. The problem can be illustrated by referring to the disruptive effect upon us when we put on spectacles that invert our vision, making us see things upside down and / or the wrong way round, so that it is difficult for us to relate ourselves to the objective realities around us in an orderly and coherent way. It takes more than a week before reorientation can be achieved when the visual and conceptual images are realigned. Only with that kind of integration is proper vision restored, and are we able to behave rationally in accordance with the objective world around us. That is the kind of reorientation that takes place when we operate with the unity of form and being, both in our knowledge of God and in our knowledge of the created universe: it involves a transformation of natural theology in its integration with our actual knowledge of God, with a conceptual reform in its mode of argumentation. Such a unity of form and being represents a return to the reconstruction of the foundations of knowledge carried through by classical Christian theology on the ground of the revealed inherence of Word and Act in the Being of God, which altered the whole concept of being in our knowledge of the world God made as well as in our knowledge of God, and which helped to give rise to the basic ideas shared by theological and natural science, now once again so prominent in our scientific understanding of the universe. Hence, when it is demanded of us in the scientific revolution of our day that we should operate in theology with the unity of form and being, or the indivisibility of the intelligible and the ontological, that demand is to be understood, not as a call to theology to submit itself to some alien way of thinking, but rather as a summons to return to its own proper epistemic basis, where, as we have seen, it has not a little in common with natural science.

If then, to follow the patristic model, we accept the inherence of *logos* and act in being, what results? We replace an abstractive and objectifying approach to knowledge by another, in which we seek to apprehend some reality or field of reality strictly in accordance with its primordial nature and integrity, i.e., under the impact of its inherent power to manifest itself as it really is and in terms of its own inherent *logos* or intelligibility. This applies equally to object-realities and to subject-realities, both of which have to be known and understood objectively in accordance with their distinctive modes of being and modes of self-disclosure. This approach has been beautifully expounded by Julian Hartt in his series of lectures entitled *Being Known and*

Being Revealed, in which he speaks of the basic features of objective being as its power to appear, to act from interior principle, and to be signified, but he also points out that our finite minds cannot match the power of signification in being itself, for it is more than we can know. This means that if we seek to know things in accordance with their own interior principles and powers of signification, instead of clamping extraneous and distorting thought-forms down upon them, we develop objective forms of thought correlated with the ultimate openness of being and its semantic reference beyond itself.

Now when we allow objective being to reveal itself to us like that out of its own inner *logos* or intelligibility, our thought is thrust up against its reality, its truth of being, in such a way that it is sustained by an objective signification beyond itself and does not fall back into the emptiness of its own inventive, objectifying operations. Not only do we grasp the truth of intelligible being out of its own depth, but we let it interpret itself to us as we develop appropriate structures of thought under its impact upon us, i.e., as we respond to its own power of signification, which bears upon our minds with categorical force. In other words, what we apprehend of something in this way, in the truth of what it is in itself, in the indissoluble unity of its form and being, *proves itself* to us by bringing our minds under an imperative obligation that we cannot rationally resist.

It is essentially a similar approach that is to be found in natural science whenever we operate with the unity of form and being or with the inherence of *logos* or intelligibility in being. Thus we seek in different fields of investigation to find ways of letting the universe disclose itself to us in its inner structure and order so that we may grasp reality in its own depth and significance—which takes place as we allow our inquiring minds to come under the compulsion of what it is in itself and its inner relations. We believe that in its own intelligibility the universe is accessible to our rational inquiry and that it is open to our articulation of that intelligibility as, in response to its impact upon us, we develop structures of thought appropriate to it. Of course these structures of thought may not be validly grounded in the objective intelligibility of the universe, that is, they may be false rather than true. But whenever we operate with the unity of form and being in scientific inquiry, we must allow reality itself to be the ultimate judge of the truth or falsity of our conceptions and statements about it. It is only when we work with a disjunction between form and being, between the intelligible and the ontological, that we find ourselves having to fall back upon some secondary criterion of truth in terms of correspondence, congruence, adequation, or merely coherence. When they are not disjoined, however, we allow whatever we seek to apprehend to force itself upon our minds by the power of what it really is in its inherent intelligibility—and thus in a way that we cannot scientifically resist. If reality proves itself to us in this way in our knowing of it, it also authenticates itself finally to us in judging the truth or falsity of our knowledge of it. We think and act scientifically under an obligation to reality, under the authority of its intrinsic intelligibility— that is what scientific conscience is about. Moreover, the more the intrinsic intelligibility of the universe becomes disclosed to our inquiries, the more it becomes evident that it is an intelligibility that stretches out indefinitely beyond our power of grasping and expressing it, so that we are aware of having to do with an intelligibility in the universe that we can apprehend only at its comparatively elementary levels. It is that indefinite range of intelligibility that gives such weight to its authority over our minds, reinforcing our awareness of the fact that in pure science we think and act under obligation to a transcendent reality over which we have no control.

Now that seems to me the situation in which St. Anselm found himself when he was engaged with the so-called ontological argument. Breaking free from the psychologism and dualism of St. Augustine, he found truth to be not only that which is what it is as it manifested itself to him, but what it had to be in his understanding and conceiving of it, for he found himself together with all created being under compulsion from beyond. It was thus, he says, that the ontological argument *forced* itself upon him from the side of what he acknowledged to be the Supreme Being or Supreme Truth, i.e., from the self-identifying reality and intelligibility of God. This is not to be understood, therefore, as the force of some logical argument or deductive or inductive train of ideas, but as the force of Reality itself, in which intelligibility and being are indissolubly one.

In St. Anselm's thought this unity of intelligibility and being characterized all created realities, so that we are under compulsion to understand and to interpret them as they really are in their own created intelligibility. But since created intelligibility is itself under compulsion from the uncreated intelligibility of God, and is thus an intelligibility that by its very nature is open to God and points beyond itself to God, that does not mean that an inferential argument may be developed from created intelligibility to the uncreated intelligibility of God, for God cannot be brought under the compulsion of any created reality or its intelligibility, as though he were indebted to it. Thus, no argument from created intelligibility, as such, can actually terminate on the Reality of God, but in accordance with its contingent nature can only break off. Hence, the ontological argument, on St. Anselm's own showing, cannot be that kind of argument either: it did not force itself upon him from created being and intelligibility, but from the Supreme Being and the self-identifying Intelligibility of God. It is, however, precisely in the coordination of those two movements of thought that the strength of the ontological argument lies, and thus in the inner connection between so-called natural theology and so-called revealed theology. The rational structure of the argumentation, when isolated and thus severed from any material content, is incomplete, and is indeed illusory, but has force only as it is completed beyond itself through integration with the actual self-revelation of God and our understanding of it under the constraint of his Intelligibility as the Supreme Being. It was in the context of prayer for that divine revelation or illumination that the argument forced itself on him from God. In other words, natural theology properly arises under the dynamic impact of God's own Being and Word, but in the context of the relation of God the Creator to the universe he has made and to the whole integrated complex of created intelligibilities that that entails.

(b) *The singularity of the universe.* Our problem here is that Western thought from ancient times in Greece has developed the habit of getting rid of singularities through some kind of scientific horror of unique events. Theories were reached by way of deduction from observations and generalization from particulars, so that scientific truths were reckoned to be universally and necessarily valid. As we have seen in discussing medieval thought, it resolved away contingence by thinking only in terms of an element of necessity that lay in any event, for it identified the rational with the necessary, and thus identified truth with logical necessity. It is basically a similar form of that age-old problem that we have in modern science when we generalize a set of ideas into a comprehensive theory and hold that the wider its generality, the more convincing it is. But here we confuse comprehensiveness with timeless universal truth and thus tend to resolve away all the singularities in the universe, i.e., to get rid of contingence.

In our day, however, singularity or contingence thrusts itself upon us in a massive way through the astonishing advances that have been made in the exploration and understanding of the universe. Much of this rests upon the inescapable singularity of the invariant finite speed of light; but since the speed of light is the constant with reference to which we ultimately define all things in the universe, including space and time, and indeed the universe itself as an intelligible whole, we have no option but to think of the universe as finite. Thus, the basic conception of the infinite universe that goes back to Newton is shattered, and the masterful place given to the concept of infinity in the foundations of science is rejected. But in this case the age-old habit of resolving away singularities or unique events into universal, timeless, and necessary truth is torpedoed. Far from detracting from a scientific grasp of the universe in its inherent intelligibility, this way of thought establishes it on a firm basis, where we have to do with what Stanley Jaki has called "the coherent singularity of the cosmos" and therewith the rise of a proper science of cosmology. The kind of intelligibility with which we have to do here, however, is contingent intelligibility, and so we are thrust back again on the Christian foundations of our science.

The problem this raises for thought is especially evident when we realize that the universe is finite in time as well as in matter and space, for that means that it had to have an absolute beginning, that it is utterly contingent on a source beyond it. Since it is not self-originating, the universe can hardly be regarded as self-sustaining or self-explanatory: and so science is up against the mystery of the universe. By its nature, science is concerned with discovering and formulating the differential laws of nature governing the processes of the universe, but it is incapable of establishing the initial conditions out of which the universe took its absolute rise and which ought surely to enter as rational equations into a full understanding of its singularity and intelligibility. The concept of the infinite universe allowed theories to develop offering explanations for its endless condition in terms of underlying necessities or unchanging homogeneities, such as theories of the "oscillating" or of the "steady-state" universe, which are evidently lapses back into the old impossible cyclic notions of the cosmos. These have, however, suffered the severest setback today on empirical, as well as theoretical, grounds, in the discovery of the $2.7°$ K microwave background radiation, universally accepted by scientists as deriving from the immense explosion initiating the expansion of the universe. We are thus all the more forcibly confronted on scientific evidence with the fact that the universe is not infinite in time and space, and we have to face up to the fact that our universe is an utterly specific and unique event.

This is something that minds of a certain type, or that

are habituated to certain modes of thought, find intolerable, for they have what Professor Alan Cook of Cambridge University has called an "obsessive horror of the unique event". It has even been proposed that, since the concept of the expanding universe, with all the singularity it implies, relies on the equations of general relativity, general relativity might be scrapped! No doubt we are up against a problem in that the closer we get to the original state of the universe before its expansion, the more inadequate physical theory based on relativity becomes. However, instead of calling for the rejection of relativity (which would be impossible, for it would invalidate a great deal of our most securely established scientific knowledge), this state of affairs would call for a profounder or higher level of physics to which our relativistic field-physics would be coordinated as a limiting case and would thus be all the more securely established on its own level and in its own immense range of reference. And that, in turn, would establish all the more impregnably the singularity or the contingence of the universe.

It is indeed rather strange to be found arguing in this way in support of the contingence of the universe, when as a matter of fact all our experimental science by its very nature depends on that contingence and would have no rational justification for its experimental mode of questioning nature apart from it. The truth seems to be that contingence is rejected neither on scientific nor on logical grounds but under the pressure of a radical secularism in our Western culture. Now to a certain extent, as we have seen, a secularizing tendency derives from the post-Reformation emphasis on the creation of the universe out of nothing— with its clear implication that we cannot know the universe out of God, for it was not created out of God, but by God out of nothing, and that therefore if we are to reach knowledge of the universe in its natural processes, we must examine what the universe has actually come to be and is and must listen to what the universe as such has to tell us of itself. Thus the doctrine of creation out of nothing gave rise to what may be called a methodological secularization, but within the context of powerful cosmological and epistemological dualisms and their deistic detachment of the universe from God, this became a *dogmatic* secularization that has bitten very deeply into our Western way of life and thought. On the other hand, secularization of this kind is itself bound to be radically undermined by the widespread acknowledgment of the contingence of the universe, within a non-dualist unitary outlook on the universe, for it forces us to ask what the universe is contingent upon, and what the sufficient reason is for this very specific and unique event, the coherent singularity of the expanding universe. That is to say, the realization of the utterly contingent nature of the universe and of its inherent intelligibility raises with us the question as to the mystery of its origin, and as to the transcendent ground on which the universe as a contingent and intelligible whole rests. By its very nature as contingent and intelligible, the universe embodies a semantic reference beyond itself, for it requires an explanation for its own intelligible state of affairs that it cannot provide out of itself.

These questions are considerably reinforced by the fact that in the continuing processes of scientific inquiry into the contingent intelligibility immanent in the universe, we find ourselves not only in a situation in which we are committed and obliged to assent to it but one in which we are taken in command by that intelligibility even when it transcends our explicit formalizations of it—and indeed any ultimate explanation we can offer of it from within the universe. It is this unbounded depth of intelligibility that is so awesome and so wonderful, as Einstein used to insist. What is baffling here is precisely the contingent nature of this intelligibility, which cannot explain itself, otherwise it would not be contingent, but which does nevertheless point us beyond itself—and yet that very pointing is something that by its very nature must break off in accordance with the contingent character of the intelligibility that prompts the pointing. Thus, while the contingent intelligibility of the universe demands—precisely on the ground of its intelligibility—a sufficient reason for it, it cannot sustain a movement of thought that actually terminates on that sufficient reason, for precisely on the ground of its contingence it precludes any necessary or logical inference to carry our thought across to an identifiable rational ground, or to God. Nevertheless, in our engagement with contingent intelligibility we are aware of coming under an imperious constraint from beyond, which will not allow us to discontinue our questioning, but summons us to be open for disclosure from the source of that constraint.

In this engagement with contingence in scientific inquiry, we are again thrust back on the original foundations laid for natural science by Christian theology. Hence, in a unitary outlook upon the universe and its intelligibility we cannot but discern a deep interconnection between scientific understanding of the coherent singularity of the universe and theological understanding of the creation. In theology we ground all our thought upon the creative relation between God and the universe, in which he not only gives it its contingent being and confers upon it its contingent intelligibility but so upholds and sustains the universe from below in its relation to himself that he provides it with that unceasing reference beyond itself to the Creator, in which its contingent intelligibility is completed and all its meaning is constituted. It is within the same created universe that natural science operates and thus within the relation of contingent intelligibility to the Creator who sustains it beyond its contingent capacities and makes it terminate on his own reality and rationality. Therefore, when scientists seeking to understand the universe in its contingent nature and intelligibility find themselves close to those zero points where their science no longer proves adequate but where they must continue to ask rational questions—not least as to the transcendent ground and sufficient reason for the coherent singularity of the universe—we must regard them as sustained and upheld by God within the ontological and semantic reference of the universe to himself as the Creator, which is the ground of that imperious constraint upon them.

This is an area of overlap in the inquiries of theological and natural science that is of the greatest significance for us today. But it is in dialogue between theological and natural science within that overlap that natural theology has its natural place. There it is concerned with the connection between the material content of our knowledge of God and the empirical correlates of that knowledge in the spatio-temporal structures of the created universe—and thus with the common concern that both theology and natural science have in the coherent singularity of the universe. What is required here is an appropriate transformation of the traditional cosmological argument, in which it will straddle and correlate the argumentative intra-structure of both theological and natural science at this point. As such, that argument can be of help to the scientist where he evidently feels the constraint of God upon him in the ontological and semantic reference of the universe beyond itself, but of help to him also with the questions he is forced to ask at the boundaries of his inquiries into the intelligibilities of the contingent universe. Again, it will be of not a little help to the theologian in unfolding and expressing the rational forms of his understanding of the relation of God to the universe as it becomes disclosed to our scientific inquiry, and not least in the development of a realist doctrine of creation as he discerns the function and fertility within natural science of the basic ideas contributed to it by Christian theology. A cosmological argument of this kind, integrated both with theology and natural science, is not a rational structure that can be treated as complete and consistent in itself, but only as consistent within the empirical conditions of our actual knowledge of God and of the creation. As such, it should have an open-structured form, enabling it to coordinate theological and scientific knowledge at this point without any reduction of one to the other.

If natural theology has its natural place in the overlap between theological and natural science where they operate within the same rational structures of space and time and have in common the basic ideas of the unitary rationality of the universe—its contingent intelligibility and contingent freedom, contributed by Christian theology to natural science—then what we are concerned with is some form of *Christian natural theology*, particularly as those basic ideas were derived through thinking out the interrelations of the incarnation and the creation. If it is objected that this is to adopt a particular and exclusive approach that lacks the kind of universality many people demand, it may be said in reply that for Christians the incarnation occupies a place of unparalleled singularity, in that it is held to be the union of the one God and a particular man in the one person of Jesus Christ. This is undoubtedly a stumbling-block for many people today, as it was for the Greeks in the ancient world, because of the horror of people then and now for the unique event. But it is precisely at this point that Christianity stands or falls, for it cannot, without ceasing to be what it is, give up the claim that Jesus Christ is the way, the truth, and the life, and that there is no way to the Father but by him.

Let me explain that claim by referring to the exclusiveness of natural law, which nevertheless has a universal range of applicability. According to Fermat's principle, a beam of light takes the minimum of time or the shortest path between two points, whatever medium it passes through. Similarly, in the formulation of a natural law the selection of one possibility as the real one thereby disqualifies the others as impossible or as unentertainable. So it is with the road God himself has taken in revealing himself to us in Jesus Christ, for once actualized in the incarnation, that reality calls into question other possibilities and makes them really impossible for us. Thus, in his concrete singularity Jesus Christ occupies for us the place of a "natural law" in the Christian faith. Nor is the term *natural law* out of place when we recall the inner connection between Christian theology and the basis of our natural science, since we entertain exclusive claims for natural law—as, for example, when the science of astronomy was established, it ruled out of court all or any kind of astrology as scientifically impossible. Far from detracting from the concrete singularity of the incarnation, a natural theology integrated with natural science as well as with Christian theology, in the way I have been advocating, can only reinforce our understanding of the incarnation even in its unique and exclusive character.

5

Theological Science

IN AN EARLIER LECTURE I tried to show that the development of Western science is profoundly indebted to three masterful ideas that were produced out of classical Christian theology, as it thought through the relation between the incarnation and the creation. Far from classical theology having been built upon the structure of science and culture, it involved a radical reconstruction of the foundations of classical science, philosophy, and religion. Classical Christian theology thus developed and took root through that basic reconstruction, which laid the foundations at the same time for the development of empirical and theoretical science as we now understand it. But while one of these revolutionary ideas, the pervasive rationality of the universe, became damaged, and the other two, the contingent rationality of the universe and its contingent freedom, became submerged and lost to view, in our day all three have been forced up to the surface again by the sheer progress of science, which shows that science as we understand it in the modern world rests upon the basic ideas produced by

Christian theology. The immense switch in our outlook upon the universe that this entails has the effect of liberating theology from the tyranny of false ideas, such as determinism and the closed universe, so that theology can now be pursued more freely on its own proper ground and can engage in deep dialogue with the science that owes so much to Christian foundations.

Today I wish to probe into the ways in which this affects the theological task in the present-day world and thus to try to show more fully how the dialogue between theological science and natural science operates. I like to think of man, especially man *qua* scientist, as the priest of creation, to which I alluded in the first lecture. Let us consider this again, in relation to the theological account given in the opening chapters of Genesis of man's place and function in the creation. On the one hand, we find that the universe is made by God in such a way that it produces life and form out of itself, each kind producing its own kind. On the other hand, we find that the universe by itself is dumb, but within the universe there is planted man, whose task it is to identify and name, that is, to bring to expression the manifold realities of the created world around him. That is, as I see it, the basic function of the scientist as priest of creation: to bring the universe to view and understanding in its inherent harmonies and regularities and thus to allow the basic design, the meaning, of the universe to become disclosed. Now man is the creature within the universe through whom the universe discloses these amazing harmonies and regularities and symmetries in its contingent intelligibility, and so is brought to speech or word, and as that happens the universe, thus unfolded and made articulate through man, constitutes a great hymn of praise and adoration to God the Creator. Regarded in this way natural science is a religious operation, for it is part of man's obedience to the Creator who has placed him in this universe and no other, and it provides the context in which we are summoned to worship and praise God.

It is in this way that theological science cooperates with what I call the new science, as the new science opens up the intrinsic structures of the universe to our understanding. But all this has a reciprocal effect upon the way in which we pursue theology, for it helps theology to be more faithful to itself as the science of God and more faithful to its understanding of the relationship of the universe to God and of God to the universe. Now in order to help us see how this operates, I would like to take three epigrammatic sayings of Einstein, in which he was wont, in characteristic fashion, to throw into sharp relief certain decisive issues.

1. "God does not play dice."

This is the most familiar of these sayings, for he repeated it frequently, usually with reference to a form of contemporary quantum theory and the idea of "indeterminacy" or "uncertainty." This had to do partly with what were called chance or random elements in nature and partly with the fact that our observational instruments prevent us from apprehending quanta irrespective of ourselves, the observers. By insisting that God does not play dice, Einstein was expressing his profound belief in the regularity of nature, but he was doing more than rejecting a view of nature as characterized by quixotic jumps. He was attacking that form of quantum theory for failing to penetrate into the inner structures of quanta and explain them in terms of field-structures and of field-laws representing them. Einstein, for his part, was accused of being a "determinist"—but that was a fatal mistake, as Pauli made clear in several letters to Max Born about Einstein's alleged "determinism." The statement "God does not play dice" rejects the idea of chance in favor of an objective but dynamic relatedness inherent in quanta. Far from being a determinist, Einstein was a realist, committed to belief in the objective intelligibility of the universe, which would have nothing to do with the Kantian idea that we can know only what we make and shape as objects of our understanding. The Kantian notion of the objectifying activity of the reason is a renunciation of genuinely objective operations, and it was that relic of Kantian subjectivity that Einstein detected and repudiated in the Copenhagen and Göttingen form of quantum theory.

In genuine scientific activity we have to do with structures in reality over which we have no control, and we try to describe them as they are, independent of our minds. Thus, for example, in the immense advances of astrophysics, we have been able to grasp something of immanent relations in the universe millions and millions of light-years before any sentient existence—let alone man—appeared. That is what science is about: man's knowledge of structures in nature independent of his knowing of them and over which he has no control, but which he knows only as he submits his mind obediently to them.

Let me express that in another way by referring to an account given several times by Michael Polanyi of an argument he had with Bukharin, in which Bukharin insisted that pure science is a disease, a symptom of bourgeois mentality, for the only science there is, is of the instrumentalist and technological kind. In wrestling with this question, Polanyi tells us, he came to the conviction that we cannot engage in genuine, rigorous science unless we have to do with a transcendent reality (*transcendent* here is Polanyi's term) over which we have no power. The truth is something over which we have no control, for in truthful relations we are in touch with objective and intrinsic structures that we may think truly only as we allow our minds to fall obediently under their power and control. That applies, of course, not only to pure science but to human rationality as such, distinguishing it from all that is arbitrary. We do not consider a person to be rational if he is unable to distinguish what he knows from his knowing of it, or if he confounds his own subjective states with objective states of affairs. In this sense, "God does not play dice," as Einstein formulated it, is a rational principle expressing the fact that true knowledge is controlled by regular and objective states of affairs independent of our conceptual constructions.

Now let us consider the application of this principle to the way in which many theologians seek to understand the incarnation—as some kind of symbolic representation of human experience of God, which has meaning for us only as it evokes or occasions certain experiences within ourselves, i.e., scientifically regarded, in an arbitrary way. Under this approach, of course, the New Testament is interpreted in such a way that Jesus is already reduced to a state of secondary significance as the symbolic objectification of a primitive religious and moral consciousness. In order to see what is going on here, and to consider it in the light of the scientific revolution that is brought sharply to expression in Einstein's saying, let me draw a distinction between prescientific thinking and scientific thinking.

Prescientific thinking is a way of thinking in pictures and images on the model of observation. Here, as in pictorial art, objects are observed from outside—for example, a sculpture, which we do not try to see on the inside but only as it appears in its surface proportions and forms, and which we appreciate as it appears to us. We operate only with a subject-object relation in which we cannot escape from things as they are seen by us—or, therefore, escape from ourselves, the beholders. We cannot get behind how things appear to us. To remain merely in the position of the subject-object relation is to remain tied to a Galilean notion of relativity. Rigorous scientific thinking, however—while retaining a place for symbolic representation—seeks to penetrate into objective coherences and structured interrelations of things as they are in themselves. Here we operate with object-object relations, or with an inherent relatedness in the field of our knowledge, in which our subject-object relations are transcended and controlled from beyond themselves by reference to the objective ontological structures of the realities being investigated. This is to operate with an Einsteinian notion of relativity.

Now regarded from this perspective, it must be admitted that not a little biblical interpretation that takes place today is still primitive in its thinking. It still works with a merely subject-object observationalist approach, interpreting the data it sifts out in terms of images and symbols, and thus it falls short of the genuinely scientific way of thinking that pierces into the inner connections that alone can control the subject-object relations in a disciplined and objective way. In scientific operations of this rigorous kind, the place of image and symbol is reduced to serve the objective, ontological reference, which is all-important. Thus, visual images have their import, not as symbolic representations of subjective states in observers, but precisely in their objective reference to the invisible and intangible realities at levels beyond appearances and observations.

If we are to think in this way, it is better not to operate with *images* and *symbols*, or similar terms, but rather to operate with the concept of analogy—but analogy must be understood in a rather different way from its traditional use, which had its roots in a Pythagorean doctrine of proportions. In scientific operations, analogical relations are not relations in which we compare things with one another on one and the same level, but are relations in which the pattern of thought or image on one level is semantically significant when it refers beyond itself to a correlate on a higher level, which may very well not be pictureable at all, but may instead be inherently unobservable, as in quantum or in relativity theory. That is the real force of analogical relations in scientific operations: the cross-level reference, in which images on one level refer to what is imageless on a higher level, but which from that higher level controls meaning on the lower level. That is how we regularly use analogical relations in the multi-leveled structures of science. This is a procedure already found in patristic theology when in an analogical or anaphoric movement of thought the iconic patterns deriving from the life and work of Christ were correlated through the incarnation to his invisible divine reality. It was a similar way of thinking at a lower level, and in the context of a Byzantine dualism, that lay behind the use of pictorial icons in worship. Many people find it difficult to think of an image as referring to what is imageless, yet that is precisely one of the important elements in the advance of scientific knowledge, which plays an essential part in both relativity and quantum theory. It is not epistemologically different when visual images in theology are to be understood to refer to imageless invisible reality beyond them as their controlling norm, even, as in relativity theory, against what appears to be the case from a primitive subject-object approach.

This transition from prescientific thinking to genuine scientific thinking, from image to inner logic, from subjectivity to objectivity, from symbolically interpreted appearances to intrinsic intelligibility, is rightly to be characterized as the transition from *mythos* to *logos*. Within the context of theology, as St. Athanasius pointed out long ago, this is a transition from *mythologia* to *theologia*, from mythology to theology. Let us consider what happens to our understanding of Christ when we think in this way and move away from the primitive observationalist approach that so regularly loses Jesus in the relativities of human subjectivity, that is, when we penetrate into the inner *Logos* of Jesus. In this approach the humanity of Jesus—far from being damaged by being interpreted as a symbol of the divine, far from being a docetic mask or mere image of divine reality detached from it—is found to be the constitutive form of God's *self*-revelation to us, the form of his *self*-giving, in indissoluble union with his own divine Being, and which is maintained as such in its perfect integrity and reality as *humanity*.

Epistemologically this approach, as we have already seen, involved in a struggle with Greek dualism a way of thinking in which the empirical and theoretical factors are held in inseparable unity. It was the bifurcation of those factors that led to the twin heresies of the ebionite and docetic Christologies and the persistence of that bifurcation that led to the contraposition of the Nestorian and Eutychian Christologies, but it was in triumph over that bifurcation that Christian theology learned to think of the incarnation, not as the coming of God into man, but of the coming of God *as man*, that is, in such a way that the oneness of God and man in Christ preserved the integrity and reality of his humanity. Thus, far from detracting from the humanity of Christ, this approach, which penetrates into the *Logos* of God incarnate in Christ and finds in that *Logos* the inner intelligibility of his incarnate reality, also finds that this humanity is preserved, and is controlled in its preservation, by that very *Logos*, for as humanity it is constituted the actual form of God's self-communication to mankind.

This has the effect of throwing us back upon the Nicene *homoousion*, which crystallized the Church's understanding of the ontological relation between Christ and God. The God whom he mediates to us through himself Jesus Christ is inherently in his own Being. And God is inherently in his own eternal Being what he is toward us in Jesus Christ. God has not communicated himself to us in Christ in some reserved way, holding back his *self*-giving so that he remains other in himself than what he is toward us in Jesus Christ. And Jesus Christ does not impart to us a communion with God which he fails to substantiate in his own Being, so that he remains finally other than God. On the contrary, there is a perfect oneness in being between Christ and God and God and Christ, so that there is a relation of absolute fidelity in God's self-communication to us in and through Christ, in which we are not deceived. Everything that Jesus Christ is of God the Father toward us is completely and finally substantiated. God is not arbitrary; he does not play dice with us in the incarnation, for the order of his self-revealing and of his self-giving in the incarnation of his Son in Jesus Christ is one which objectively exists and is dynamically operative in his own eternal Being. Thus, to allow a theological interpretation of Christ within the context of the scientific approach carries us back to the heart of classical Christology.

2. "God does not wear his heart on his sleeve."

The import of this saying overlaps with that of the saying we have just been discussing, but here we have a somewhat different emphasis. If "God does not play dice" stands for Einstein's conviction that there is an immanent order everywhere in the universe—an ordered regularity of all events independent of us—"God does not wear his heart on his sleeve" stands for the conviction that the real secrets of nature, the reasons for that order, cannot be read off the patterns of the phenomenal surface. That is to say, we cannot deduce from appearances the deep structures of reality. In science Einstein's concern was to penetrate into the underlying ontological structure of the ordered regularity of things, to which the phenomenal patterns of that regularity are coordinated, and by which they are controlled, and in reference to which they may be accounted for.

At the risk of tedious repetition, let me try to explain this a little more, for it is very important. I sometimes conduct a little experiment in class, holding up a book and asking what shape people see. Almost invariably I get the answer "a rectangle." Actually, however, you do not see a rectangle and could not, for the angle of your perception could not be adjusted to the face of the book in such a way as to make that possible. What you do see is some sort of trapezium. Or take a coin: from whatever angle you look at it, you do not see a perfect circle, but only some elliptical shape. Yet you know that the face of the book is rectangular and the face of the coin is circular. In each case you operate with an invisible structure, intuitively or intellectively apprehended, that controls the appearance of the object and makes you see it as it really is, rectangular or circular. But you cannot derive the idea of the rectangle or the circle by deducing it from the appearance of the thing. Yet that is the defective thinking found among positivists who speak of deducing ideas from appearances, or among some biblical scholars who claim to provide the theologian with critically tested observational data from which he may deduce theological ideas.

Let us be quite clear. In scientific thinking we do not reject the Galilean principle of relativity; we do not reject the fact that we are observers who operate inescapably with appearances and images relativistic to themselves as observers. We all engage in primitive subject-object experience. Observational images, therefore, have a place in our thinking, but they are reduced to a minimum, for they are intersected, as it were, by the pattern of relations at a deeper level by which they are objectively controlled and made to refer beyond themselves. Scientific thinking and understanding moves to that deeper level, refusing to rest content with the surface patterns of observational experience. To be rather technical for a moment, what we are concerned with here are the invariant yet dynamic objective structures of the space-time metrical field, which, though inherently invisible and intangible, control all observational phenomena. Hence, we do not offer explanations deduced from appearances, but we explain why things appear in such and such a way from their objective grounds. That is why scientific theories are not *argumenta ad hominem*, but are grounded upon deep object-object relations that hold good on their own, independent of appearances and observations. Thus in scientific thinking we are not concerned with appearances as such, but with objective structures in the light of which we understand appearances, and we do not consider that we can understand objective structures from appearances. Now here we have a *bouleversement* of the observational approach that is part of the profound revolution in scientific outlook in our day, in which biblical scholars and theologians have not yet fully participated, and of which they seem often quite unaware!

The patterns of events on the surface of experience are, then, relative to the observer, but on dualist assumptions that means that we can never ultimately reach knowledge of the real world beyond us, or what is called the external world. That is why on dualist assumptions we can never reach knowledge of Jesus Christ. We can only reach knowledge of the appearances of Jesus: interpreted appearances, that is, in the consciousness of the primitive Church—but of course on the same dualist assumptions even that is to be questioned, for we can only reach knowledge of those interpreted appearances as they appear to us and not as they are "in themselves" in the consciousness of the primitive Church! If we reject dualism, however, we operate with an inherence of form in being, which leads to very different results. Here we have to do with the intrinsic, imageless, constitutive structure of things, which is invariant through relativity for any and every human knower, and which cannot be grasped by observational means, but only through intellective penetration or theoretic insight. While outward shape on the surface of things remains observable and imageable and is variant for every observer, the imageless, invisible structure remains constant and invariant for all observers.

Thus, while we are empirical beings—embodied minds, if you like—in a physical universe characterized by rationality, we have always to think in such a way that the empirical and theoretical factors bear upon each other. This does not mean that we operate with "facts" and then with interpretations put upon "facts," for we only have facts that are inherently significant, that have inherent intelligible relations, and thus an inherent meaning, in virtue of which the facts are what they actually are, and in the light of which they are to be understood. That is to say, we reach knowledge in such a way that the surface of things is coordinated with deep, invisible structures; we think empirical and theoretical levels of reality conjunctively together in a dimension of ontological depth. "God does not wear his heart on his sleeve."

And so we think again of Jesus Christ. He is not to be understood by trying to fit him into the surface patterns of other "phenomena." Try as you will, for example, to interpret the Virgin Birth or the Resurrection of Jesus by fitting it into the patterns of other phenomena on the same level, you will not make sense of it. But it does not make sense either to think together the kind of connections we derive through an experiment in quantum mechanics and the kind of connections we operate with in setting up that experiment—namely, connections that obtain in Newtonian mechanics—*on the same level*, for then we reach only absurdities and contradictions. That does not mean that quantum theory is absurd. On the contrary, it means that quantum theory is so rational and so objectively grounded that the kind of connection that obtains in Newtonian mechanics has to be broken and limited to its own level if it is to remain valid. That is how we have to think scientifically in a universe that discloses itself as multi-leveled in its rational structure. Why should we try to think otherwise of Jesus Christ? If we try to fit him into the patterns of other phenomena on the same level, we lose him in the relativities of man's observational experiences. Only by penetrating into the non-observable intelligible reality of Christ, only by penetrating into his essential *Logos*, which is constitutive of his incarnate actuality, may we grasp Christ in his wholeness and inherent force. But here we must learn the discipline of thinking conjunctively together his human-historical and divine-eternal aspects or levels, and must thus think of him from the start as at once human and divine—one indivisible, whole reality.

In the multi-leveled or cross-leveled thinking that this approach involves, particular attention must be paid to the way in which the same concepts and terms are used on different levels, for they inevitably suffer change through their integration with the kind of connection that obtains from level to level. For example, *space* as used at our ordinary level of day-to-day experience and speech differs considerably from the scientific use of *space* at its different levels. Hence, in rigorous scientific thought we try to use concepts and terms with precision, as they are defined by their place in some logico-deductive or syntactical system as well as by their semantic or ontological reference, so that we are prepared for a significant switch in meaning of the same concepts and terms as we move from level to level. This is especially important when we move from the level of ordinary—i.e., prescientific—knowledge and experience in which observation plays a powerful role, to scientific levels, for the basic concepts and terms that arise at the level of our prescientific observations, even when they naturally involve an integration of empirical and theoretical elements, need to be changed, and sometimes drastically, if they are to be adequate for scientific knowledge. That applies no less to theology than to natural science. To refer to Athanasius once again, he pointed out that theological terms need to be elastic, for they are stretched by the realities to which they are used to refer and are thus changed from their common use. Unless that takes place, they cannot be used to convey what they are intended to convey in the reference from one level to another beyond their original level of use.

Now if the levels are separated from one another, as takes place on dualist assumptions—so that the empirical and the theoretical ingredients of knowledge split apart and are treated as separate levels—then we lapse back into primitive, prescientific thinking and are imprisoned within observational concepts and the picture-thinking that belongs to them. So far as Christology is concerned, this involves two clear consequences. On the one hand, thought about Christ bifurcates into the old ebionite and docetic approaches, one empiricist and the other rationalist. On the other hand, the theological models that are developed tend either to be "picturing models," which have only symbolic value, or "theoretic models," which claim to have explanatory value.

If, however, we operate not on the ground of dualist

assumptions, but with the ontological integrity of the unity of form and being and therefore with cross-level references that are also of an ontological kind, then something very different arises. As already noted, theology of this kind penetrates into the essential *Logos* of Christ, which is not only constitutive of his incarnate actuality but must, as such, be allowed to control our knowledge of him even in respect of the empirico-observational relations that obtained between him and others. Here then, as we think his human-historical and divine-eternal manifestations conjunctively together in the unity of his one person, we develop in our knowledge of him, not "picturing models" built up out of observational images nor "theoretic models" built up out of our *a priori* conceptions, but what we may call "disclosure models."

A "disclosure model" in natural science is a conceptual construct forced upon us by the intrinsic intelligibility of some field as we inquire into it, and it is developed as a theory through which we seek to let the structures of that field disclose themselves to us. A scientific theory is a compound question that we put to a particular field, and that we refine and adapt in the light of the answers we receive. But that is a progressive operation, for the theory or model is progressively changed and refined in the light of what becomes disclosed. A scientific theory or model of this kind is a sort of lens through which we allow nature in its intrinsic patterns to reveal itself to our apprehension. In the process of refining the lens or the theory, our basic images and concepts undergo radical change; otherwise they would be opaque and not transparent media. Moreover, in this refining process, as our theories or models advance from level to level in a deeper grasp of reality, we find operating the analogical or cross-level references in which images are made to refer beyond themselves to imageless objective structures by which they themselves are controlled in our knowledge.

All this applies, *mutatis mutandis*, to theology and the development of disclosure models in Christological inquiry. These models are intellectual structures that arise in our knowledge as we seek to let our minds and hearts fall under the self-disclosing power of Christ through his *Logos*, in such a way that all our "images" of him are steadily refined and made to refer imagelessly to what he is in his intrinsic significance: thus as "images," and certainly as observational "images," their place is reduced to a minimum. Far from being a picturing model then, a disclosure model of Christ is one in which, not the representative, but the referential element is primary, for it functions only as an instrument for the progressive self-revelation of Christ to us. Far from being a theoretic model, the disclosure model of Christ does not seek to explain, for example, *how* he is constituted in the hypostatic union of his divine and human natures, but serves as a theological instrument through which we allow Christ in his own mystery and reality to impose himself upon our apprehension of him, so that we know him more and more out of himself and his intrinsic significance.

For a disclosure model of this kind let me refer to the famous Chalcedonian formula of 451 A. D. It fulfilled a rigorous scientific function in setting aside the Nestorian and Eutychian Christologies, which developed from the bifurcation of the empirical and the theoretical approaches, but instead of seeking to impose some new theoretic structure upon Christ, it formulated a frame of reference directing the Church to Christ in such a way as to allow him in his undivided reality and mystery to go on revealing himself to their worshipping apprehension. Determinate statements beyond what was knowable were ruled out, so that as a disclosure model it calls for further and further refinement in the light of deepening knowledge of Christ reached through it. The tragedy of the Chalcedonian formula in the history of thought is that it soon became caught in the rising tide of Byzantine and Augustinian dualism, already evident in the teaching of Leo the Great; and it was from that dualist interpretation of Chalcedonian Christology that John Philoponos was castigated as "monophysite." But the ancient Chalcedonian formula can be resurrected today and reinterpreted in a non-dualist framework of thought in which it can fulfil a rigorous scientific role that could be, I believe, of even greater significance than ever before.

3. "God is deep but not devious."

This is my rendering of a saying of Einstein's that is more literally translated as "God is sophisticated but not malicious." If "God does not wear his heart on his sleeve" is intended to express the idea that the secrets of nature cannot be read off its phenomenal surface, "God is deep but not devious" expresses the complexity and subtlety, yet the ultimate simplicity and reliability, of the universe. That is to say, the immanent order hidden behind the intricate and often baffling interconnections we find in the universe is essentially *trustworthy*, for—in spite of all that might appear to the contrary—when we come up against sets of events for which there seems no rational explanation, the universe is not arbitrary or evil. God does not play tricks with us.

Since the universe is utterly contingent in its nature

and contingent even in the kind of intelligibility intrinsic to it—and what is more, is characterized by a contingent freedom—it is not surprising that there should be so much in the universe that baffles our attempts to bring order into our understanding of it; nevertheless, we operate in all science with an ultimate and unshakable belief in its rationality and reliability. Take the subatomic realm, where scientists find fluctuations that seem to tell us that we are up against something quite random and arbitrary, of which we have difficulty in making sense by, for example, the classical laws of thermodynamics. Yet even here these fluctuations have been yielding up their hidden intelligibility, which can be brought to rational expression in open structures and systems. Thus our belief is reinforced that, in all the astounding manifestations of nature and in the fluctuations that we are not able adequately to understand, the universe remains reliable. God does not play tricks with us.

Think of the remarkable place that light occupies in modern science. Hermann Weyl once said of Einstein's theory of relativity: this means that light occupies a unique metaphysical status in the universe. If—to be technical once more—all bodies in motion are relationally defined with reference to space and time, all space and time are relationally defined with reference to light and its velocity. But undefined by any reference beyond itself, light is the great *constant*, with reference to which ultimately all else we know in nature is relationally known and defined, and upon that constant we can invariably rely. That is why Einstein insisted that, for all his intricacy, God is not devious: he does not deceive us. Throughout all the dynamic, multivariable structures that pervade the universe of bodies in motion, somehow this constancy of light has always supported the conviction that God—in our sense, not Einstein's sense—does not play tricks with us. God does not let us down.

Let us think for a moment of the patristic doctrine of light. The Fathers used to stress the fact that while we cannot look into the sun or source of light, we do see what is lit up by light. This is something we understand even better today: that light itself is invisible. Several years ago when visiting Dundee University I was taken round the metereological station to see photographs of the earth that were coming in from a new artificial satellite orbiting the earth. I asked to be showed the jet where the stream of light signals came in that gave the information about the weather. I saw nothing coming out of it, and so held up a piece of paper in front of it and immediately there appeared a spot of light on it. The light itself I could not see, but I could see what was enlightened by the light. That is true even of the sun itself—it is not the sun's light that we see: we see what is lit up by light in the sun. That is something the Fathers were constantly saying, certainly on good Biblical grounds: it is in the light of light that you see light, and they applied that to God. God is Light, uncreated Light, and it is in the light of that invisible, uncreated Light that the created lights of the world are visible. Thus, we understand the rationalities of nature, or what I have called its contingent intelligibility, in the light of the uncreated Rationality of God. You understand created light in the light of uncreated Light. It is because God's Light is constant that we believe in the ultimate stability and reliability of the universe which he has correlated to his Light. So here we have a remarkable analogy between the unique metaphysical status of physical light in the contingent universe and the unique status of the Light that God is, from a theological point of view.

Here we have a problem, with which Einstein, at this point at any rate, does not seem to have reckoned. When we take the statement "God is deep but not devious," which expressed his conviction that throughout the physical universe there is an order of a trustworthy and reliable kind, and generalize it to comprehend all human existence and experience, we find that it does not take account of evil, pain, error, and sin—that is, of darkness, disorder, and irrationality in the world, which, face to face with God's self-revelation in Jesus Christ, we know to conflict with his divine will and love. What are we to make of that?

First, let us recall the biblical emphasis, especially strong in the Old Testament (to which I alluded earlier in discussing creation), on the goodness and faithfulness of God, which yields a view of the created world as good and orderly, with a reliability grounded beyond itself in the sovereign rule or commanding Word of God. This is particularly evident in the Psalms, where we find the overwhelming conviction that—in spite of the evil and pain and disappointment and disaster that overtake even godly and righteous people—in the unrelenting faithfulness of God, the divine order of righteousness and goodness will prevail; that is, the order that lies behind all creation, manifest even in the regularities of inanimate and animal existence, which are subject to the majestic Word of God. But where is this conviction stronger than in the Book of Job, in which we hear that the goodness and righteousness of God will not allow Job to compromise his faith in the face of the devastating disasters that overwhelmed him—far less to give up in cursing skepticism and despair? In spite of all the evidence that shouts aloud to the contrary, Job is unable to escape the overwhelming power of his conviction that everything is ultimately ordered, though often quite inscrutably, by the good will and purpose of God, who is completely trustworthy. "Though he slay me, yet will I trust him."

Let us reflect further on this notion of *order*—here again we are not without a significant parallel between theological and scientific thought. Take the statement "There is order in the universe"—I am thinking here of the way in which Alastair Mackinnon of McGill University has discussed this in his fine book *Falsification and Belief.* This statement expresses one of those beliefs upon which all science relies. If there were no order in the universe, there would be no science, no rational knowledge whatsoever. That is not to say that there are no inscrutable elements in our experience—that there are not sets of events of which we can make no scientific sense—but that in spite of all this, we remain convinced that there is order in the universe. Nevertheless, that there is order in the universe cannot be proved, for to "prove" it, we have to assume it—just as we cannot "prove" the laws of logic without assuming them to do so. This is an ultimate assumption of science, then, which is both unverifiable and unfalsifiable, yet we cannot give it up without plunging into irrationality.

Suppose in the course of some piece of scientific investigation we come up against some events in nature that we cannot construe in any scientific way so as to make rational sense of them; we do not cast away our scientific outlook and insist that the world of nature is irrational. On the contrary. It is precisely because we hold unshakably that there is order in the universe that we refuse to believe that there is ultimately anything irrational about these events. Somehow the intelligible pattern latent in them has eluded us, but we continue to interrogate the events until that pattern becomes clear, in the light of which we can understand them.

We have similar experiences in common everyday life. Take a shocking event such as the death of a little child through cancer, and the terrible cry of the heartbroken mother: Why? Why? How could God allow such a thing? And in her bitterness she gives up her faith in God. But does she? It is only because in some deep contradictory sense she does believe in God as the God of love and order that she is so rebellious. Her belief in God makes her revolt with all her being against this evil fact, this disorder in the world, for it is an attack upon the love that God is. That God is love is not something that we can verify or falsify. It is like the ultimate beliefs in science upon which all else depends and in the light of which everything we know in the universe is construed. That God is love is the ordering force behind the creation and operative in all God's providential government of created existence. Everything ultimately depends on it. We cannot give up the conviction that God is love, therefore, without plunging into irrationality and despair, so that we seek by reference to the love of God to make what sense we can of the dark disorders of our world, for they cannot be the ultimate word to the enigma of existence—yet we remain baffled.

But what of the order of redemption in which again everything depends on the love of God? Here is something for which we have no evident counterpart in natural science: the incarnation in our world of the very *Logos* or Word of God by which all things were made, which is a movement of the ultimate love of God penetrating into our world in a creative reordering of it from within. As such, the incarnation is not an intrusion or an interference in our creation—as though the love of God were alien to it or the creation were alien to the ordering rationality of God revealed in that love. The incarnation is the deep ontological intersection of the patterns of our world by the divine order of love—that is, the intersection of patterns that have somehow gone wrong and have become twisted in disorder—in order to inject into them a reordering at a deeper level. Hereby the disturbance and violence and lawlessness of our world are transfixed and taken in command in such a way that they are made—in spite of and against what they are in themselves—to serve the ultimate triumph of the love of God over all. But this intersection of our disorder and irrationality and evil by the divine order of love incarnate in Jesus Christ necessarily involves the atoning passion of God in Christ, by which our disordered existence is restored to order even in its ontological foundations beyond anything that the creation is capable of in itself or anything that could be conceived by us. The sheer presence and passion of God himself in the Cross—with its intersection of our darkness by God's light, our evil by God's goodness, our irrationality by God's rationality, our disorder by God's order—tells us that ultimately, behind all the chaos and lawlessness of our existence in the universe, there is no irrational enigma, but only the creative and regulative purpose of God's love. The God who confronts the world in the crucifixion of Christ is deep but not devious. He is Light, and in him there is no darkness. He remains ever constant and invariant in the perfect Law of his own eternal Being, ceaselessly faithful to his eternal purpose to set up within our world the invincible order of his love, which is a creaturely reflection of his own inner divine order.

Theologically, this tells us a good deal about the bearing of the incarnation upon the creation and about the inseparable interrelation of the incarnation and the atonement, but I do not propose to pursue that now. Rather, I wish at this point to direct attention to the question of how we are to relate the divine order of redemption through God's ordering love to the kind of irrationality and disorder disclosed through scientific inquiry—not so much in the physical sciences as in the human sciences. We are up against complex problems here. I find myself facing this sort of problem at a different level when I try to understand modern music. I am not a musician, although I love music, but what I find difficult to appreciate is the modern way of resolving dissonance; the result seems to be not much more sometimes than a clever ensemble of musical events in which, theologically speaking, there is no forgiveness of sins, no absolution, since dissonance remains, although it is made to serve another pattern of musical events. Looked at from the scientific point of view—and I suppose one can in a measure apply science to art and music—what we have here may be expressed in this way (suggested to me by André Mercier), as the intersection of symmetries, the breaking of a symmetry on a lower level by a symmetry on a higher level. Dissonance appears to remain, but it is opened out through a cross-level integration in which the effect given is of a richer texture and a deeper level of musical order. If this is the case, I would like to extend it to bring in the role of counterpoint, in which case we would think of the *canto firmo* as calling the broken symmetries of the lower level into such contrapuntal relation to it that they are given a harmony beyond what they are capable of in themselves at their own level alone. If we take these two musical concepts together, we may get some sort of analogy to help us understand our problem concerning how the symmetry of the ordering love of God breaks into the apparent symmetries of our life with all their harsh dissonance, and by breaking those symmetries, it not only breaks up the dissonance they entail, but takes them up, redeems and transforms them in a profound ontological reordering of the whole.

In this intersection of the divine symmetries with those of our existence in this world, we are made acutely aware that God is Light and there is no darkness in him, that God is Love and there is no dissonance in him, that the activity of God is always an ordering activity and there is no disordering element in it; but we are also made acutely aware that the intimate linking of our world to such a God through the incarnation and resurrection of his Son inevitably thrusts our world forward into a future very different from any that can be read off its observational patterns. The breaking of the active and redemptive divine order of Light and Love into the spatio-temporal patterns of our existence is bound to be at once eschatological and teleological. As the divine symmetries break into the patterns of our estranged existence, they have the double effect of cutting short their dissonant, disorderly forms and of restoring them to their true forms in the creative purpose of God in such a way that they are now directed forward through space and time to a consummation in the ultimate victory of God's love. This must be taken seriously, for by the very nature of the incarnation and resurrection with their indissolubly empirical correlates in space and time, we are theologically bound to relate the future prospect of the universe, given to it through its redemption in Christ, to the understanding given to us, under God, of the created realities of the universe as they become disclosed to us in the process of scientific inquiry—otherwise we would lapse back into a dualism that divorced redemption from creation.

Let us consider the place of *prediction* in scientific activity. There are two kinds of prediction. One kind of prediction, which I call "improper," is merely a deduction from one set of determinate events that we already know to another and similar set of events of which we were unaware. But that is not a genuine prediction, for we are not thereby directed to any new events or ideas, but only to those events and ideas already latent in the body of our knowledge, which through logical analysis and deduction are now brought out into the open. Moreover, since these events and ideas are necessarily connected with what we already know, this kind of prediction operates only with a closed determinist system: there are no open possibilities. Such is the kind of prediction put forward by the positivists.

In a proper prediction, however, we are really concerned with open possibilities. Since the empirical and theoretical elements in what we seek to know are inseparably intertwined, we cannot reach new knowledge through theoretical means alone; and since the universe is contingent in nature, we have to rely upon experimental science, in which we let the universe itself provide us with answers. In this case, any true scientific theory formed under the pressure of the intelligibilities immanent in the field under investigation, any theory that really bears upon reality in its ontological order in this way will indicate more than it can express in its actual formulations at the time; and since the objective intelligibility of the space-time world reaches out far beyond and ahead of us, true scientific theories bearing upon it are bound to have a future or predictive reference. Nevertheless, while scientific predictions of this kind may well point us in the direction in which we believe new knowledge will arise if the theories concerned are true, when we actually make the discovery it takes us by surprise. It turns out to be more than we have, or could have, predicted. Since it arises, however, in an intelligible universe as well as a contingent one, any possible discovery will be one that can be assimilated with our prior knowledge through a rational reconstruction of its basis, although it could not be logically or necessarily derived from it. Thus, a true scientific theory will have a fertile character corresponding to the spontaneous power of the contingent universe constantly to disclose itself to us in unexpected ways in the future. It is indeed the fertility of a scientific theory, manifested in its capacity to open up unexpected problems as well as new aspects of reality, that is taken as a hallmark of its truth and acceptability. Prediction of this kind, then, is a usual element in scientific knowledge of a universe that is characterized both by contingence in its intelligibility and freedom and by the vectorial character of its space-time structures.

True theological knowledge and statement are in this respect not dissimilar to scientific knowledge and statement. Although they are grounded in the intelligibility of God through his self-revelation and are not arbitrary inventions on our part, they have to do with God in his unlimited reality and are therefore also correlated to open possibilities—but as such they cannot be theoretic constructs logically deduced by us. Insofar as God reveals himself to us and we come to know him and speak about him through the medium of the spatio-temporal structures of the contingent universe, the forms theological knowledge and statements take will participate in the vectorial character of those structures, and so on that ground alone they will have a future reference. But the ultimate ground for their predictive character is their bearing upon God himself. In that they bear upon him in his infinite transcendence over all time and history, they must have an eschatological quality in a reference through time and history to the future; and since that future is not arbitrary, but is bound up with the ultimate purpose of God's love revealed in Jesus Christ, they will also have a teleological quality in being geared into the consummation of that purpose. It is this double aspect of their eschatological and teleological character that is distinctive of prediction in theological knowledge and statement. If they were only teleological, it might be possible to develop some sort of calculus of possibilities in prediction; if they were only eschatological, they would break off without any clear predictive reference even in indicating more than they can express. Nevertheless, even though they are both eschatological and teleological, any true prediction they entail would be so correlated to the inexhaustible freedom and spontaneity of God both in creation and in redemption that its fulfillment could only take us utterly by surprise—as Jesus himself kept on insisting.

If we are not to lapse back into a dualist bifurcation of creation from redemption, we must relate scientific prediction and theological prediction together in some way, for the future of the universe in the redemptive purpose of

God's love is not to be divorced from the design of the universe, or therefore from the future of the universe, as understanding of the universe and its design is unfolded through man's scientific exploration of it, for that very scientific exploration is itself an integral part of the expanding universe and of its unfolding design. If it is man's function within the universe to be that element constituent in it whereby the universe produces understanding of itself, it is that same man in his God-given relation to the universe who is given through the incarnation of the Son or Word of God an inescapable place in the ultimate purpose of all creation. Indeed, as St. Paul expressed it, all creation is in a sort of travail, in an agony of anticipation, as it reaches forward to the fulfillment of man's place in the universe as a child of God. That "theological future" and the "scientific future" must somehow be correlated in a meaningful way, in which damage is done to neither prospect but, rather, in which each is deepened and enriched.

This understanding of man's place in the universe from the perspective of God's ultimate purpose may be helpfully related to some questions that have recently begun to engage attention in the scientific perspective. When we contemplate the unitary rationality of the space-time universe—the intrinsic coherence of its balanced adaptations and organizations in the exchange of matter and energy that continuously takes place within it—and reflect on the remarkable development of order through mutation and adjustment, our minds are naturally carried forward to the thought of its *end*. Here something else thrusts at us from behind the predictive possibilities, namely, the "purpose-like" functioning of its immanent processes and the proleptic character of the whole movement of expansion. It is as though its immanent processes had been programmed in such a way as to lead up to the emergence of man, and beyond. This question is not one that can be suppressed on scientific grounds. As J. A. Wheeler has remarked, "No longer is it possible to throw the question out as meaningless, though it is stranger than science has ever met before" ("The Universe as Home for Man," *American Scientist*, Vol. 61, no. 6).

Here we have to do with what Sir Bernard Lovell has called, in his recent work, *In the Center of Immensities* (1978), "a most remarkable and unsuspected entwinement of man with the actual existence of the universe and of time and space" (p. 110). He goes on to point out that our very presence in the universe today requires it to have certain properties. "At least one essential condition of our existence is that the Universe must expand at almost precisely the rate at which we measure it to be expanding. If the rate had been less by an almost insignificant amount in the first second, then the Universe would have collapsed before any biological evolution could have taken place. Conversely, if the rate had been marginally greater, then the expansion would have reached such magnitudes that no gravitationally bound systems (that is, galaxies and stars) could have formed" (p. 113). That is to say, if the rate of the expansion of the universe had been marginally greater or less, the emergence of life would have been impossible. Does this mean that the universe was proleptically conditioned from the very start by the eventual emergence of man? In Professor Wheeler's words (from the article above) "Has the universe had to adapt itself from its earliest days to the future requirements for life and mind?" Evidently it does not seem rationally possible in a scientific understanding of the universe to keep man himself out of the picture, for he is himself not only a constituent element in the universe, without which the universe as we know it would not be what it is, but the highest form of existence in its expansion. In this event, we can hardly keep out of the picture man's own intellectual and religious development either, in which purpose and transcendent reference to his intelligible ground in God are essential.

At this point we may turn to another significant development in recent scientific thought, the extension of thermodynamic theory to the presence in the universe of spontaneous order, creatively arising out of given initial conditions. Classical thermodynamics is concerned with entropy, or the degree of disorder in equilibrium (i.e., closed) structures or systems. The second law of thermodynamics concerns the irreversible increase in the measure of disorder or disorganization in such structures or systems. On the other hand, it is a fact that the evolution of the universe in its orderly developments, and above all in the rise of biological structures, manifests increasing measures of organization and order. Now, however, through the work of Ilya Prigogine and others, we have been given an extension and application of the second law of thermodynamics beyond its classical frame of reference to take in also non-equilibrium (i.e., open) systems in which order spontaneously arises out of apparently random fluctuations far from the state of equilibrium in such a way that closed systems obeying the laws of entropy on one level are coordinated with open systems at a higher level characterized by a minimum of entropy (the least dissipation of energy) and are for this purpose controlled by them at their boundary conditions, to yield what Michael Polanyi had called "stable open structures or systems." It is evidently this hierarchical coordination of levels that throws much light upon evolution in the expanding universe: higher and higher levels of organization and order emerge that rest on the basis of physico-chemical relations at a lower level obeying thermodynamic law. Thus in the expansion of the universe new forms of coherence and order continuously appear. This applies, of course, to the highest form of life on earth, man himself, for within the natural scientific perspective he is to be regarded as the product of such spontaneous or self-organizing order. But in this event it applies no less to the personal and social structures of life that he develops—although it is only too frequently evident that in some of his behavior (and where more than in politics?) the second law in its classical form applies only too vividly, for the output of disorder seems to be in strict proportion to the input of order! For example, Sir Bernard Lovell, in the book to which I have just referred, reminds us that our "efforts to redress the balance between the rich and the poor nations through modern science and technology have not merely failed to do so, but have worsened the situation substantially" (p. 153). It is doubtless in the light of the laws of entropy that one must also consider the irrational and disorderly elements in human existence we discussed earlier, but that is the obverse of the point we are concerned with here, that man himself is to be understood in the light of the same principle that governs the coordination of the open-structured connections at a higher level with the determinate structures at a lower level. In accordance with this principle, man must be regarded as one whose level of rational existence and order is to be understood only if it is coordinated with a higher level beyond him, i.e., with a transcendent level in God's interaction with him in the space-time track of the universe which, as we have had occasion to note, is never a disordering, but only a creatively ordering, activity.

Certainly from a theological perspective it is in man—as man of science and man of faith: the creature who, in Karl Barth's terminology, lives on the boundary of two worlds, the visible and the invisible, the earthly and the heavenly—that the symmetries in the divine order of things intersect and give substance and meaning to the otherwise quite ambiguous purpose or end latent in the intelligibilities of the expanding universe. In this intersection of the cosmic symmetries by the divine symmetries, we can begin to understand why the "purpose-like" character of intramundane functions and processes is so ambiguous: they are correlated to the unlimited spontaneity and the infinite freedom of God—his "infinite differentiality," as it were—and only come into clarity in coordination with his eternal purpose; yet this very coordination keeps them open and indefinite, so that when they are regarded in themselves they can be spoken of only as "purpose-like." The sheer contingency of the universe—it might well have been otherwise; it may turn out to be other than it appears from our "predictions"—is not abrogated but deepened, so that scientific understanding on the mere level of contingent process will never be able to give cosmic symmetries a necessary and determinate interpretation if it remains faithful in its thought to the contingent nature of the universe. They will always retain their baffling ambiguity for science, precisely in virture of their sheer contingence. This, incidentally, is why science cannot operate with *final causes*, for that would import a closed and determinist universe, denying its ultimate contingence—as happened with medieval Aristotelian science.

It may also be remarked that since theology, even when properly grounded in God's self-revealing interaction with the world, remains a human inquiry, operating within the contingent intelligibilities of space and time that it shares with natural science, it is also characterized by ambiguity in its formalized concepts and statements. By their contingent nature they fall short of the divine realities they indicate, pointing far beyond themselves to what is infinitely greater than we can conceive or express; God cannot be brought into any compulsive relation to our concepts and statements about him. True theological concepts and statements are at one and the same time geared into the intelligible relations they intend and cut short in themselves as no more than human concepts and statements. That is precisely what we have already noted in the remarkable blending of the eschatological and teleological ingredients in our theological understanding of the saving purpose of God in respect to the created universe and its final consummation. While the teleological ingredient derives from the incarnation, or the embodiment of God's eternal purpose of love in space and time, the eschatological ingredient relates to the fact that the fulfillment of that purpose cuts across and outruns all our expectations, for it is correlated to the infinite differentiality in the relation of God to the creation.

To return to the interconnection between natural scientific and theological understanding of the purpose of the created universe, we may express it like this. The stratified or hierarchical structure of levels of order and coherence revealed by scientific inquiry—in which prediction and vectorial thrust forward to an intelligible end are present—

is set within a semantic focus toward God the Creator and Redeemer, which provides those levels of order and coherence with a significance beyond what they are capable of in themselves, but which completes what they are in themselves. At the same time, this also serves to coordinate theological understanding of an eschatological and teleological consummation with the development of scientific inquiry, or rather with the active unfolding and developing of the expanding universe as it comes to formed expression in our science. If man is the constituent element in the universe whereby the universe knows itself, then the development of the scientific understanding of the universe is an integral part of the process of the expanding universe. How very much this turns upon man as the priest of creation in the fulfillment of the role given him by the Creator, both as man of science and as man of faith.

What have I been trying to do in this lecture? I have not tried to show that Christian theology is based upon the new science and its remarkable opening of the universe; but that even if we succeed in trying to think theologically within the paradigms of the new science, along lines suggested by Einstein's intriguing sayings, we find ourselves driven back to the great truths of classical Christian theology that we have already reached in different ways, on the proper ground of God's self-revelation. If we interpret that self-revelation, however, within the context of this scientific revolution, far from finding it a menace, we find that our basic Christian convictions are clarified and fortified and are given an even deeper relevance to the exciting world that daily opens out to our scientific inquiries.

6

The Basic Grammar of
Theology

IN THIS LECTURE I would like to discuss the relevance of
the kind of approach we have found being forced on us
to the doctrine of God. In the great change that has taken
place in the foundations of knowledge, we have learned that
genuine knowledge in any field involves knowledge of that
field in accordance with the nature of the realities with
which we have to do in it, and knowledge of those realities
in terms of their internal relations or intrinsic structures.
How does this affect a formulation of the doctrine of the
Holy Trinity?

Before answering that, let me recall what happens under the old dualist approach, where we operate within a
context of epistemological and cosmological dualism. We
found that this involves a doctrine of the immutability and
impassibility of God, and what I called a deistic disjunction
between God and the universe. Hence, when we try to

relate God to the universe, we do so in terms of what science has come to call an inertial system. That is equally true of the medieval approach with its doctrine of the Unmoved Mover and the Newtonian approach with its notion of God as impassibly or inertially containing the universe through his absolute time and space. It is also true, of course, of the so-called "process theology" with its doctrine of the "Moved Unmover," as Colin Gunton speaks of it. Now within the context of the old dualist approach, there takes place a radical bifurcation in the doctrine of God. We noted the difficulties produced by Newton's bifurcation of the role of God in relation to the world he had made. But in traditional theology, above all in Roman Catholic theology, dualism leads to a bifurcation between the doctrine of the One God and the doctrine of the Triune God, so that Roman Catholic theology regularly produces two separate treatises, *De Deo Uno* and *De Deo Trino*—for example, in the two treatises of Lonergan under these titles, which have now been produced in English.

It was this basic split in the concept of God that troubled Karl Barth and prompted him to attack the division of theology into natural theology and revealed theology, when natural theology is taken to be the ground of the doctrine of the One God and revealed theology is taken to be the ground of the doctrine of the Triune God. As we have already had occasion to note, this involves basically the same problem as that which arose between Euclidean geometry, conceived as an antecedent conceptual system on its own, and physics, or the actual knowledge of the universe. Barth rejected any idea of a natural theology in the form of a "preamble of faith," as Roman Catholic theology calls it, and so he rejected any doctrine of the One God developed apart from and antecedent to the doctrine of the Triune God, for that would posit a schizoid state of affairs in the very foundations of theology. Basically the same bifurcation is to be found in much Reformed theology, and especially in Westminster theology, with its bifurcation between a covenant of works and a covenant of grace, which yields the same result in the doctrine of God.

What happens when we do away with dualism and the bifurcation in our basic approach and in our basic concepts that it inevitably involves?

If God is triune in his nature, then really to know God means that we must know him in accordance with his triune nature from the start. It is certainly scientifically objectionable to develop a doctrine of the Trinity on ground other than that on which we develop our actual knowledge of God, the One God. But further, if we operate, not with some kind of epistemological dualism between form and being or structure and substance, but with the unity of form and being or of structure and substance, then to know God we must know him in accordance with the form or structure of his own Being—that is, in terms of God's inner divine relations. And that means we must know him as the Triune God who within himself has relations between Father, Son, and Holy Spirit; so that for us to know that God, we must know him in a mode of understanding on our part appropriate to the Trinity of Persons in God. There must be a "trinitarian" character in our knowing of God, corresponding to the trinity of relations in God himself.

Now that was the great insight of St. Augustine: but it will not do on Augustine's dualist approach to operate with a trinitarian structure that we have in our minds, independent of or apart from our actual knowledge of God, as he claimed, for example, in the statement that there is an image of God in the mind of man even apart from its participation in God. That would be to develop an independent, conceptual structure of psychological relations in human nature, in terms of which we interpret the doctrine of the revealed God as we meet him in the revelation of Holy Scripture. A similar mistake, of course, is regularly to be found in modern theology of the phenomenological or sociological or psychological types. Now it is precisely this Augustinian dualism, still lurking in our theology, that we need to get rid of, whether in its medieval Thomist or Aristotelian form or in its Protestant Newtonian form—or its phenomenological offshoots.

It is instructive here to ask what is done by Jews, who do not believe that God is triune as Christians do. This is rather an exciting question to ask, especially after the great work of Martin Buber, and not least in the light of the fact that Jews are forced to relate God—the living, acting God—to suffering, forced upon them not only by the fearful experiences of Jews in the European holocaust, but by the experiences of Israelis in the Holy Land today. Buber saw through the problem of modern Protestant thought very clearly when he attacked it for what he called its "conceptual letting go of God." That conceptual letting go of God was the result of the Kantian dictum that we cannot know things in themselves, but only as they appear to us in their external relations, which means that we cannot even know Jesus, let alone God, as he is in himself, for it destroys the cognitive character of faith. Actually, however, we grasp things in our thought, and hold them in our thought, only if we can grasp them in their internal relations. Think of a mountaineer trying to climb up the face of a rock cliff: if it is sheer and utterly smooth, without any cracks in it, it is impossible. Unless he can get his fingers or spikes into the rock, and thus make use of the interstices or intrinsic relations in the rock, he cannot grasp hold of it. How then could Martin Buber claim to grasp God and not let him go conceptually if he is the ineffable, unnameable God of Judaism? Would not his grasp slip off the sheer face of the undifferentiated oneness of God? At this point Buber's thought appears to be covertly trinitarian, in his appeal to the relations of love within the Being of God himself—which he took over from Spinoza, whose doctrine of God's rational love of himself within himself had been influenced by Christian thought. There is a kind of meeting of love, a profound reciprocity, within God, and it is when our knowledge of God latches on to that internal relationship deep in God that we can really conceive him and know him in accordance with his intrinsic nature. And that is the ground, as Buber showed, for a conceptual grasp of God. That is just what we are concerned with in classical Christian theology, in its radical difference from post-Kantian neo-Protestant theology (for example, in Paul Tillich), which operates with what is called a nonconceptual relation to God (not a signitive, but only a symbolical, relation to God, in Tillich's language), meaning, of course, that the cognitive content in what is called knowledge of God derives, not from faith in God, but from some aspect of human culture.

Now let us move on and ask how we are to approach the self-revelation of God and the self-giving of God mediated to us in the New Testament Gospel; and how we are to appropriate knowledge of him for ourselves within the context of the scientific revolution in the foundations of knowledge, in accordance with which the dualism between the empirical and the theoretical has been abolished—and likewise therefore the bifurcation between form and being, or structure and substance. We develop our theological inquiries, then, in movements of thought in which we seek to know God strictly in accordance with his nature, and in terms of his own internal relations as they become disclosed to us through the incarnation.

Let us take our starting point here from Athanasius, reverting again to his doctrine of the *enousios logos* and *enousios energeia*, to which allusion has already been made. *Enousios logos* refers to the Word/Reason inherent in the *ousia*, or Being, of God; *enousios energeia* refers to the activity or movement of power inherent in the *ousia*, or Being, of God.

a) If God's *Logos* inheres in his own Being eternally, and that *Logos* has become incarnate in Jesus Christ, then it is in and through Christ that we have cognitive access into the Being of God, into his inner divine intelligibility or *Logos*. There is a parallel to this, as we have had cause frequently to see, in the way we now seek to understand nature, or the universe, in accordance with its internal rational order or intrinsic intelligibility. Hence we speak of apprehending natural realities in terms of their intrinsic structures, or, if you like, in terms of their intrinsic reason. In developing his account of this, St. Anselm actually spoke of an *intima locutio*, an intimate locution embedded in being—in created being in its contingent way and in the Supreme Being or God in his transcendent way. And that is right, for in theology particularly the *logos* is not simply intelligibility or reason but word—it is a locution, a rational speech. With God, *Logos* is the mode of the divine Rationality expressing himself in Word.

b) If God's *energeia*, or "act" inheres in his Being, and that act has taken the form of Jesus Christ in the incarnation, so that he is identical with the action of God (and thus identical with the eternal decision or election of God), then we know God in accordance with the acts of his Being, in accordance with his activity in disclosing himself to us. In this respect also we may point to a parallel in science, in the great switch from static to dynamic categories, and underlying that in the switch from a static to a dynamic way of understanding the universe, that differentiates the medieval from the modern world, evident in the immense stress on experimental operations, which are the appropriate kinds of questions we direct to a dynamic universe. This is the switch in the thought of God that process-theology seeks to make, and that must be appreciated as such.

Here we have to reckon with a two-fold distinctiveness in the operations of theological science as compared with the operations of natural science, scientifically forced on us by difference in the nature of the subject-matter in the field of theological inquiry, namely, God himself.

a) That God's *Logos*, or Word, inheres in his Being means that God's Being is speaking Being, eloquent Being. He is not Being which also speaks, but Being which speaks precisely as Being, for his Being and his Word interpenetrate one another and are inseparably one. Hence, there can be no thought of knowing God in his mute Being, as it were, apart from his Word, behind the back of his eloquent Reality as God, for there is no such god.

b) That God's *energeia*, or Act, inheres in his Being, means that God's Being is in his Act and his Act is in his Being. He is not Being which also acts, but Being which acts precisely as Being, for his Being is intrinsically active, dynamic Being. Hence, there can be no thought of knowing God in his Being stripped of his Act, behind the back of his Act, or apart from his active Reality as God, for there is no such god.

Contrast what this means with our inquiries in natural science. In natural science we direct our questions to nature in order to let nature answer for itself by disclosing itself in its inner relations, so that we know it or grasp it as we let our minds fall under the power of those inner relations. We speak of nature as "answering" our questions and "disclosing" itself to us through the "speech" of its inner intelligibility, but this is somewhat figurative language, for actually nature is dumb: it cannot talk to us. While we do our best to listen to nature, it is we who have to turn its mute signals into word and bring its inner patterns and structures to expression in the form of theories and laws. Since it is tempting to us to make nature say what we want, we devise means to obstruct ourselves from that kind of imposition upon nature, but there is no doubt that what must predominate is a spirit of respectful humility before the astonishing intelligibility of nature and a childlike readiness to open our understanding to whatever nature may reveal of itself.

In theological science the formal scientific requirements are not really different from this, but in this case we direct our questions to the God whose very Being is eloquent with Word, and whose Being bears upon us with his creative activity. Here we have to do with the living God who reveals himself to us in such a way that he creates in us the capacity to receive and apprehend him; and he communicates himself to us in such a way that he lifts us up into the inner communion of his divine Being so that we are given to share in the mutual knowing of the Father and the Son in the Holy Spirit and thus to know God as he is in himself in the immanent relations of Father, Son, and Holy Spirit. Further, this God reveals himself to us and communicates himself to us where we are in our error and wrong and sin, in our misunderstanding and self-centeredness, in such a way as to strike into the very heart of our being and to turn us inside out, in order to redeem us from sin, reconcile us to himself, and assimilate us into the communion of love in his triune Being. That is why the divine revelation penetrates into our inquiries, takes the initiative in questioning us, and so turns our questions upside down and inside out, reshaping them creatively under the impact of his eloquent Being. This is very different from what happens in natural science, for here we are up against the sheer majesty of the living God and his uncreated Word, and are summoned to listen in a way in which no scientist has to listen to the summons of nature. Here we have an objectivity profounder than any objectivity that natural science has to do with, for we are face to face with the Creator of the universe itself, encountering us as himself Word and Act, who cannot be mastered by us, but who remains in his transcendent Reality the Lord over all our questions, before whom we are at the bar, questioned down to the very roots of our being.

Such is our vocation in Christian theology: it is a kind of ecstatic passion, in which—under the sheer impact of God's own Being in Word and Act—we are called to think of and to know him, not from a center in ourselves, but from a center in God, in such a way that it cuts across the grain of our natural desires and mental habits and creatively reorients them. In it we have to do with the eloquent and dynamic Being of God himself, whom we may know only in accordance with the steps he has taken in revealing himself to us and the steps he has taken in reconciling us to himself, through the incarnation of his Son within the ontological structures of our human existence in this world, in such a way that he sets up within it the laws of his own internal relations and our rational understanding takes on the imprint of what it is given to know, the triune Reality of God himself. To know this God, who both condescends to share all that we are and makes us share in all that he is in Jesus Christ, is to be lifted up in his Spirit to share in God's own self-knowing and self-loving until we are enabled to apprehend him in some real measure in himself beyond anything that we are capable of in ourselves. It is to be lifted out of ourselves, as it were, into God, until we know him and love him and enjoy him in his eternal Reality as Father, Son, and Holy Spirit in such a way that the Trinity enters into the fundamental fabric of our thinking of him and constitutes the basic grammar of our worship and knowledge of the One God.

I am not concerned now with the content of this triune knowledge of God, but with the way in which our knowing of God and the formulating of our knowledge of him operate within the context that has occupied our thoughts in these lectures. When we reflect on it in this scientific way, we find that our knowledge of God as Triune reveals a stratified structure on the ground of God's self-revelation to us—which is the actual ground on which our knowledge of God arises—not unlike, formally at any rate, the stratified structure that we develop in a rigorous scientific account of our knowledge in any field of investigation. And, incidentally, this stratified structure bears some relation to the historic stages in the formulation of Christian knowledge of God as we find it in the rise of classical Conciliar theology.

Let me describe this stratified structure—and let me say I have in mind the account given of this kind of structure in physics by Einstein in his great essay entitled *Physics and Reality*.

1. First, we have our basic level of experience and worship, in which we encounter God's revealing and reconciling activity in the Gospel. This takes place, not privately, but within the context of the life and mission of the Church: that is, along with others who share with us this common experience. Its focal point is encounter with Jesus Christ within the structures of our space and time—and therefore within the structures, rationalities, and objectivities of our subject-subject, subject-object, and object-object experiences in this world—where we are summoned to live and act as intelligent beings who are part of the intelligible but contingent creation.

This basic level I call *the evangelical and doxological level*, for it is the level of our day-to-day worship and meeting with God in response to the proclamation of the Gospel and the interpretation of the Holy Scriptures within the fellowship of the Church. This is a level in which, as we would expect, empirical and theoretical factors are inseparably interwoven with one another (the level of incipient theology), so that—from the very start of our experience and knowledge—form and being, structure and substance, are indivisibly united in the realities with which we have to do and in our rational and experiential response to those realities.

2. Then we come to *the theological level*. As we direct our inquiries to God in this field of evangelical and doxological experience, we find that he reveals himself to us as Father, Son, and Holy Spirit, in a three-fold movement of his love in revelation and redemption, in which we come up with certain basic concepts: that is, "Father," "Son," and "Holy Spirit." They are concepts of three distinctively personal modes of divine activity and ways of being, but they are more than modes, for the mode is inseparable from the reality of which it is the distinctive mode, or way of being— Father, Son, or Holy Spirit. This is the level in which we speak of "the Economic Trinity": the level in which we are concerned with the Act of God in his Being, with the personal acts of God in his personal reality as Father, Son, and Holy Spirit. The term *economic* was the patristic expression for the orderly way in which God communicates himself to us within the structures of space and time, in which he remains what he is eternally in himself while communicating himself to us really and truly and without reserve in Jesus Christ and in his Spirit.

3. We come to a *higher theological and scientific level*, in which we penetrate more deeply into the self-communication of

God in the saving and revealing activity of Christ and in his Spirit. At this level we are explicitly concerned with the epistemological and ontological structure of our knowledge of God, moving from the level of economic trinitarian relations in all that God is toward us in his self-revealing and self-giving activity to the level in which we discern the trinitarian relations immanent in God himself which lie behind, and are the ground of the relations of, the Economic Trinity—that is, we are lifted up in thought to the level of "the Ontological Trinity" or "the Immanent Trinity," as it is variously called. This is the movement of thought in which we are compelled, under pressure from God's self-communication, to acknowledge that what God is toward us in the three-fold economic activity of his revelation and redemption, as Father, Son, and Holy Spirit, he is antecedently and eternally in his own Being in the Godhead. This is the passage of thought from the Trinity *ad extra* to the Trinity *ad intra*, as theologians say. While from an epistemological perspective we speak of moving from a lower level to a higher level in which (as indeed in all rigorous scientific activity) the higher controls the lower, in reality the Economic Trinity and the Ontological Trinity are identical, for there is only one divine Reality of God in himself and in his saving and revealing activity toward us in this world. It is the Trinity in this ultimate, ontological sense that the great theologians of the early Church such as Athanasius, Gregory of Nazianzus, or Cyril of Alexandria identified with the subject-matter of theology par excellence. In the strictest sense the doctrine of the Holy Trinity is *theologia*, that is, theology in its purest form, the pure science of theology, or *episteme dogmatike*. I myself like to think of the doctrine of the Trinity as the *ultimate ground* of theological knowledge of God, the *basic grammar* of theology, for it is there that we find our knowledge of God reposing upon the final Reality of God himself, grounded in the ultimate relations intrinsic to God's own Being, which govern and control all true knowledge of him from beginning to end.

The decisive point for theological science lies here: where we move from one level to another—from the basic evangelical and doxological level to the theological level, and from that level to the high theological level of ontological relations in God. This is undoubtedly the great concern that occupied the mind of the Council of Nicea when the Credal formulation it produced, in spite of fiery discussion, clearly arose out of a profound doxological orientation. It was written by the Fathers, so to speak, on their knees. Face to face with Jesus Christ, they had to do immediately with God, who so unreservedly communicated *himself* to them in Christ that they knew Christ to be the embodiment of God, so that they not only worshipped God through and with Christ but in Christ, worshipping God face to face in Christ who is himself the face of the Father turned toward them. Jesus Christ the incarnate Son is the God whom they worship in the ontological mode of his personal *self*-communicating in the flesh, so that in their union and communion with Christ they are in union and communion with the eternal God.

It is, then, within this profound reciprocity between God and man established by God's incarnational self-communication to us, that our movement of epistemic reference from level to level takes place: from the level of evangelical and doxological experience and understanding to the level of an integrated grasp of the economic relations in God's activity toward us, and from that level to the level of our understanding of God as he is in his own intelligible relations. It is on the ground of the *hypostatic union*, the indissoluble union of God and man in the one Person of Christ, that the epistemic reference we make can have any substantiation in reality, for it is through that hypostatic union in Christ that such a reference is firmly anchored in the reality of God and of man. Such an epistemic reference is an actual sharing on our part—through the Communion of the Spirit, who dwells immanently both in the Father and in the Son—in the unique and closed mutuality not only of knowing and loving but also of being between the Father and the Son. The Son does not know the Father as the Father knows himself, nor does the Father know the Son as the Son knows himself without their being of one and the same Being. That relation in Being, the consubstantiality between the incarnate Son and the Father, the Council of Nicea expressed by the term *homoousios*: Jesus Christ is confessed to be God *of* God, of one and the same Being with God, the very one who for us men and our salvation was made *man*. The *homoousion*, then, to refer to it in its more abstract form, is of staggering significance. It crystalizes the conviction that while the incarnation falls within the structures of our spatio-temporal humanity in this world, it also falls within the Life and Being of God. Jesus Christ is thus not a mere symbol, some representation of God detached from God, but God in his own Being and Act come among us, expressing in our human form the Word which he is eternally in himself, so that in our relations with Jesus Christ we have to do directly with the ultimate Reality of God. As the epitomized expression of that fact, the *homoousion* is the ontological and epistemological linchpin of

Christian theology. With it, everything hangs together; without it, everything ultimately falls apart.

Epistemologically the *homoousion* stands for the basic insight that we derive under the creative impact of God's self-communication upon us—that what God is toward us in his saving economic activity in space and time through Christ and in the Holy Spirit, he is antecedently and eternally in himself. The focal point is Jesus Christ himself. In the cross-level reference from the basic level to the theological level, the insight takes the form that what Jesus Christ is toward us in love and grace, in redemption and sanctification, in the mediation of divine life, he is inherently in himself in his own Being—he is not different in himself from what he manifests of himself toward us in his life and work. But in the cross-level reference from the second to the third level, the insight takes the form that what God is toward us in Christ Jesus, he is inherently and eternally in himself in his own Being—he is not different in himself from what he manifests of himself toward us in Jesus Christ. This means that our experience of God in Christ is not somehow truncated so that it finally falls short of God, but is grounded in the Being of God himself; it means that our knowing of God is not somehow refracted in its ultimate reference, but actually terminates on the Reality of God. In fact, of course, this movement of reference on our part is grounded in the movement of God himself condescending in the free outpouring of his love to be one with us in the incarnation of his Son, and in and through him to raise us up to share in his own divine life and love which he eternally is in himself. That is what the *homoousion* expresses so succinctly and decisively.

Let us pause for a moment to take a side-look at the

epistemological counterpart to this in natural science, as that may help us to grasp more firmly the significance of the *homoousion*. In natural science this is the point where we part company with Immanuel Kant, for here we are concerned with penetrating through the level of our empirical and early theoretical understanding of reality into its internal relations, for if nature is not in itself that which we claim to know of it in its relations toward us, then we do not really know nature but are merely operating with convenient symbols or useful arrangements of observational data. This is the decisive point of Einstein's critique of the phenomenalist and Kantian approach to knowledge, when he broke through it and grounded scientific knowledge on the objective intelligibility of the universe: that is, upon an inherent relatedness that characterizes the universe independently of our perceiving and conceiving of it. This all-important point, theologically speaking, may be called the *homoousion* of physics(!), the basic insight that our knowledge of the universe is not cut short at appearances or what we can deduce from them, but is a grasping of reality in its ontological depth, and that we are unable to pierce through appearances and apprehend the structures of reality unless we operate with the ontological integration of form and being, or of structure and matter, which is, after all, what $E = MC^2$ entails. Nature does not deceive us or play tricks with us, for—as inherently in itself what it is toward us in our inquiries—it is everywhere trustworthy and reliable. Thus the *homoousion* of physics represents an epistemological revolution of very far-reaching significance for natural science.

This movement of thought in physics, however, does not allow us to project appearances, as such, back into things in themselves, for it comes at the appearances from behind in such a way that we can control the distortion that affects things in their appearances relatively to the observer. Thus the *homoousion* of physics involves a critical operation in which we discover what not to read back into things in themselves, while nevertheless correlating what we know of things as they are disclosed to our inquiries with what they are in their internal relations. No more does the *homoousion* of theology allow us indiscriminately to read back into God all that we know of Jesus in the flesh, for that could easily lapse into some form of mythological projection into God of what is human and finite. A critical edge enters into the *homoousial reference*, especially from the second to the third level, in the movement of thought from the economic activity of God toward us in space and time to what he is ontologically or immanently in himself. Here in theological science, as in other scientific activity, we develop devices in which we obstruct ourselves from projecting our own subjectivities into God or from confounding God known by us with our knowing of him. It belongs, of course, to the essence of rational behavior that we distinguish objective states of affairs from subjective states of affairs, and thus constantly distinguish what we know from our knowing of it. This is not always easy. Since God makes himself known to us within the modes of our creaturely and human reality (as in the incarnation above all) there is an inevitable and proper element of anthropomorphism in our knowledge of God—this makes it all the more imperative, however, that we learn how to distinguish what is properly anthropomorphic from what is improperly anthropomorphic in our knowledge of him. God reveals himself to us through establishing a relation of reciprocity between himself and us in which he condescends to use human modes of thought and speech, but in this reciprocity God relates himself to us as Lord and Savior, the Judge of our wrong and the Forgiver of our sins, so that there is a continuous critical moment throughout his relations with us in which he distinguishes himself from us. This is the context in which we must operate with a rigorous criticism of all our anthropomorphic ways of thought, submitting them to the judgment of the divine Majesty, and as we do that we learn to discern and to reject what is improperly anthropomorphic. There is no time to discuss this more fully now, but it may be pointed out that it is at this point that theology brings into play the analogical relations we have already discussed, in which iconic images taken from Christ are made to refer to what is imageless in God: that is, in which our anthropomorphic images are critically controlled by the objective, intelligible relations in God himself.

Before we go further, let us ask what we are to say of the Holy Spirit, whom we believe to be no less than the Father and the Son of the Holy Trinity. It is evident that the *homoousion* must also be applied to our understanding of the Holy Spirit, although in a manner appropriate to his personal mode of Being. What the Holy Spirit is toward us in the divine acts of recreation and sanctification in Christ, he is inherently in himself in God. He is so inwardly and essentially related to the very Self of God in his self-giving and self-communicating that the Holy Spirit is revealed to be of the same being as the Giver and not some gift detached from God or some created emanation from him. The communion with God that the Holy Spirit is toward us—as through Christ he gives us access in himself to

God—he is in his own Being as God. He also is God of God, of one and the same Being with the Father. But there is a proper difference in our use of the *homoousion* of the Spirit from our use of it of the Son. The Son is, as the Word, the mode of Being in which God utters or expresses himself; and it is in the incarnation of that Word that God has expressed himself to us. But that takes place within the structured objectivities of our created world in such a way that an epistemic bridge is established in Christ between man and God that is grounded both in the Being of God and in the being of man. Hence in Christ the *homoousion* is inseparably bound up with the *hypostatic union*. Thus the incarnation of the Son or Word constitutes the epistemological center in all our knowledge of God, with a center in our world of space and time and a center in God himself at the same time. It is in and through that Word that we have cognitive access to God and to knowledge of him in himself.

It is by reference to this epistemological center in the incarnate Son—that is, to the *homoousion* of the Son and the *hypostatic union* in him—that we also clarify our knowledge of the Spirit, who is not knowable in his own personal mode of Being in the same way, for he is not embodied, like the Son, in the concrete realities and structured objectivities of our world of space and time, or like him, therefore, brought within the range of our human knowing at our created level. He is God of God but not man of man, so that our knowledge of the Holy Spirit rests directly on the ultimate objectivity of God as God, unmediated by the secondary objectivities of space and time through which God is revealed in the Son, and it rests only indirectly on those objectivities through relation to the Son with whom he is of one Being as he is with the Father. Throughout all God's self-revelation to us in the incarnate Son, the Holy Spirit is the creative Agent in mediating knowledge of God to us in himself and the creative Agent in our reception and understanding of that revelation, although he is not himself the Word of that revelation or the Form which that revelation assumes as it comes from the Father and is appropriated by us. But because it is in the Spirit as the immediate presence and power of God in it all that we know God in this way, the Father through the Son and the Son from the Father, we know the Holy Spirit in himself as Lord God no less than the Father and the Son, who with the Father and the Son together is worshipped and glorified. It is through holding constantly in our thought the inseparable unity between the economic activity of God in the Spirit and his economic activity in the Son that we may be prevented from reading back into God himself the material or pictorial images that arise out of the reciprocity he has established with us though the incarnation of his Son in space and time, for through the oneness of the Son and the Spirit the iconic images of God in the Son are made to refer imagelessly to God.

Through the application of the *homoousion* in these ways, appropriate to the Spirit as well as to the Son, our thought is lifted up from the level of the Economic Trinity to the level of the Ontological Trinity; and in the process of this cross-level reference we reach the refined concepts and relations by which we seek to express the ultimate constitutive relations in God, in virtue of which he is who he is as the Triune God. Let us be quite frank. To speak like this of God's inner Being we cannot but feel to be a sacrilegious intrusion into the inner holy of holies of God's Being, before which we ought rather to cover our faces and clap our hands on our mouths, for God is ineffable in the transcendence and majesty of his eternal Being. The God whom we have come to know through his infinite condescension in Jesus Christ, we know to be infinitely greater than we can ever conceive, so that it would be sheer theological sin to think of identifying the trinitarian structures of our thought and speech of God with the constitutive relations in the Being of the Godhead. All true theological concepts and statements inevitably fall far short of the God to whom they refer, so that their inadequacy, as concepts and as statements, to God must be regarded as essential to their truth and precision. The Triune God is more to be adored than expressed.

This does not mean that when we reach this point, at the threshold of the Trinity *ad intra*, theological activity simply breaks off, perhaps in favor of some kind of merely negative or apophatic contemplation, for the sheer rationality, as well as the majesty of God's self-revelation, will not allow us to do that, but summons us instead to respond in rational thought and speech in ways that are *worthy* of God.

Two comments seem to be called for here, before we move on.

a) The movement from economic to ontological relations in God must be taken seriously, for in Jesus Christ, the embodiment of God's eternal Word, we are in touch with real, intelligible relations immanent in God. Even though by their ineffable nature they defy anything like complete formalization, they are the ultimate constitutive relations in God, which by their internal perfection are the ground upon which the intelligibility and objectivity of all our knowledge of God finally repose, and as such they play a role of unifying simplicity in all theological doctrines.

b) Any formalization we make in a movement from the second to the third epistemological level—from an ordered account of the economic activity of God toward us as Father, Son, and Holy Spirit to an ultimate set of fundamental concepts and relations whereby we seek to reproduce in thought and speech the ultimate constitutive relations in God—can be done only at the expense of substituting highly attenuated relations for the concrete relations of God's self-revealing and self-giving through Christ and in the Spirit. Hence, we may engage in this movement of theological thought if we allow the concepts and relations we employ to supposit for real relations, or, more simply, if we steadily hold to the identity of the Ontological Trinity with the Economic Trinity.

Let us return now to the question of how the three theological levels we have been considering are structured and coordinated with one another, thereby leading us to this supreme point in the knowledge of God in his internal intelligible relations. In order to help us here, let us take another side-look at what happens in physics—where we are certainly operating with a very different field of reality, but where we are concerned to engage in careful scientific procedure. I take my cue again from Einstein's essay *Physics and Reality*, in which he offers an account of the different strata or levels of knowledge in a scientific system: the level of ordinary experience, and the loosely organized natural cognitions it involves; the level of scientific theory, with its search for rigorous "logical" unity; and a third level, where we develop an even stricter and higher "logical" unity with a minimum of concepts and relations. Theoretically this process of raising our thought from one level to a higher level is indefinite: it goes on until we reach a level where we can operate with a set of ultimate concepts and relations as few as possible, but with the greatest conceivable unity. In actual practice, however, three levels—which Einstein calls the primary, the secondary, and the tertiary—are normally sufficient to enable us to reach a unified conceptual grasp of reality in the field of our investigation.

At the ground or primary level of daily life, our experiences and cognitions are naturally and inseparably combined together. Here our basic concepts are intuitively derived and are directly correlated with the complex of sense experience. Naturally, the outlook in all this is realist, for as rational beings we operate instinctively with a belief in the reality of the external world independent of our perceptions.

When we move from this realm of ordinary thought close to experience to the secondary or scientific level, we seek to order the basic concepts in our understanding of the real world by connecting them up into a theory, in the process of which we shed what we judge to be unnecessary, or merely peripheral, cognitions and ideas. The purpose of such a theory is to enable us to penetrate into the interior connections in reality that ground and control our basic experiences and cognitions. The concepts and relations that we deploy at this secondary level are not immediately connected with our common experience, for they are refinements and extensions of the basic cognitions bound up with it; their function, however, is to enable us to grasp and to understand common experience from the intelligible relations intrinsic to it, but which are not themselves directly experienced. Hence, the concepts and relations we develop on this level are useless abstractions unless they are compatible with our ground experiences and cognitions, so that empirical correlation with them is essential. In the effort to organize our basic concepts and relations at this level into a proper theory, we bring in certain ideas that we have creatively thought up under the constraint of reality, and that are therefore intuitively correlated with reality, and we deploy them as freely chosen fluid axioms through which we develop the theorems needed for coherent and consistent formulation of the theory. These theorems turn the set of basic concepts and relations, thus organized, into a problematic theoretic structure through which we may question reality and grasp its intrinsic structures more effectively than we could without it, but which by its very nature is revisable in the light of what becomes disclosed through it. But if the theory is consistent, it is incomplete, and its consistency depends on cross-level reference to relations on a higher, or meta-scientific, level, where again we must seek to order our thoughts round the basic concepts and relations into a tighter and more rigorous formulation.

As we move from the scientific level to this meta-scientific level (or second scientific level), we seek to deepen and simplify the organization of basic concepts and relations developed at the scientific level. This will involve the revision and clarification of the theorems already used, to test their compatibility with experience, and the formalization of a higher and more rigorously ordered theory, in which theoretical connections that played a significant and useful role at the lower level may well have to be discarded as no longer necessary. This higher-order theory will also have to be put as a question to reality and to be clarified, revised, and simplified accordingly. Thus we reach the ultimate theoretic structure characterized by logical economy and simplicity (i.e., with a minimum of conceptual relations), through which we grasp reality in its depth as faithfully as we can, and which we use as the unitary basis for simplifying and unifying the whole body of our knowledge in the field in question, in the course of which not a little of it will disappear as of only a temporary nature and finally irrelevant.

Relativity theory is the most striking example of a higher-order theory of this kind characterized by logical simplicity and comprehensiveness. In reaching the idea of relativistic invariance, Einstein devised a mathematical form of invariance as a theoretic structure or conceptual instrument through which he could discern and grasp an inherent relatedness in the universe. This mathematical invariance is not to be identified with the objective invariance in the universe, but is relativized (in the other sense of the term) by it and is revisable in the light of it. Thus in relativity theory we have to do with one of those ultimate structures in nature and in science that constitutes a rational basis for the unification and simplification of knowledge. Regarded in this light the stratified structure of a scientific system appears like a sort of "hierarchy of truths" (to transpose to science a theological term from the Second Vatican Council), which is pyramidal in shape—for from a broad basis, scientific inquiry advances through levels of increasing logical rigor and simplicity until it reaches the ultimate set of a minimum of intelligible relations in terms of which, as its ultimate grammar, the whole structure is to be construed, each level being reckoned the limiting case of the one above it, in reference to which, however, it reaches its own consistency and truth.

That is the side-look. What happens, then, in the scientific formulation of the doctrine of the Trinity? The decisive point, as we have seen, is located in Jesus Christ himself, and our understanding of the relations inherent in him, i.e., the hypostatic union in connection with the *homoousion*, in which the two natures in Christ himself on the horizontal level, as it were, are interpreted in the light of the vertical or cross-level reference in the *homoousion*. It is by entering, as far as we may and can, into the inner relations of the Word and Act of God in Jesus Christ himself that we get the basic clues to our movement of thought from level to level—which is a movement of thought remarkably similar to what we have just been considering in natural science. Here in theology also we operate with new ideas, freely created under the impact of God's self-revelation, such as *hypostatic union* and *homoousion*, but the one I wish now to consider is the idea of *perichoresis*. This word derives from *chora*, the Greek word for "space," or "room," and indicates a sort of mutual containing or mutual involution of realities, which we speak of as a *coinherence*. This concept was first formulated like a "fluid axiom" (to use a modern term from meta-mathematics), to help us discern and grasp the way in which the divine and human natures in the one Person of Christ interpenetrate each other without the integrity of either being damaged by the other. In the course of this, forms of hypotethico-deductive arguments were also employed to clear the ground, but not to establish the connection, in order to clarify and give consistency to the interconnection of the concepts being used, but not to impose any kind of logical necessity upon it. That is to say, theological understanding of Christological concepts was organized and ordered as clearly as possible at this level.

Theological understanding then pushed to the higher level through the Economic to the Ontological Trinity by means of the *homoousion* and the notion of *perichoresis*. But now this notion is refined and made to refer to the mutual interpenetration of the three Persons—Father, Son, and Holy Spirit—in one God. Once *perichoresis* is refined and changed to apply to the Trinity, however, it can no longer be applied to Christology at the lower level, to express the union between the divine and the human natures in Christ, without serious damage to the doctrine of Christ. Whenever that has been done in ancient or modern times it has resulted in some form of a docetic rationalizing and depreciation of the humanity of Christ. On the other hand, it is in connection with the refined conception of *perichoresis* in its application to intratrinitarian relations in God that Christian theology developed its onto-relational concept of the divine Persons—or rather, an understanding of the three Persons in the one God as onto-relational realities in God. And of course this gave rise to the new *concept* of *person*, unknown in human thought until then, and to the onto-relational notion of person at that, which is applicable to our interhuman relations in a created way, correlated to the uncreated way in which it applies to God.

It is highly significant that the doctrine of *person* thus reached is not logically derived, as in Western thought—Roman Catholic or Protestant—by way of individualization of rational nature (as in the famous definition of Boethius), but is ontologically derived from the Communion of Being in Love in God himself. This understanding of person was picked up in the West by Richard of St. Victor in the twelfth century, was remarkably expounded in his *De Trinitate*, and had a theological tradition through Duns Scotus down to Calvin, but there is no need to pursue that, except to say that this understanding petered out in Western thought in face of the atomistic, individualistic thinking of Locke. In view of all that, it is worth noting that Greek patristic thought had already taken its measure of atomistic modes of understanding the relations between human beings as individuals who are only interconnected through their external relations, and it was in the course of their Christian reconstruction of ancient culture that the onto-relational concept of the person was produced. That was undoubtedly a great achievement, for—difficult as this onto-relational way of thinking has been for the Western mind—once the concept of person, both as applied to God and as applied to man, was introduced, it had the widest and profoundest impact, not only on the West, but upon world thought and culture.

But why is this onto-relational way of thinking difficult for us? It is not because it is inherently difficult, but because of the long-ingrained habits of mind and of speech with which we are beset in the Latin-Greek tradition of Western culture, and the static connections with which we have been accustomed to operate in our linear logic. But the onto-relational way of thinking is not difficult for people in some other cultures. The Bantu, for example, naturally thinks in relational ways, so that the concept of onto-relational thought would not be difficult for him. But onto-relational thinking is difficult for us because of the impact of atomism, ancient and modern, in our culture. That is why we find the same problem arising in physics when science had to switch from thinking only in terms of particles and their external relations to thinking in terms of dynamic and continuous fields.

In our own day, modern particle theory and quantum theory have been forced to develop something like onto-relational notions—for example, where we find that the interrelations between particles as space-time entities, or dynamic energy-knots, are as significant, if not more significant, than the so-called particles. Thus within the indivisible connection of particle and field, we operate not with discrete particles, but with onto-relational realities which we find it rather difficult to bring to precise expression in our traditional subject-object predicate language and its grammar, not to speak of its logic.

Let me illustrate the problem by reference to some correspondence I had several years ago with a physicist of London University, Fritjof Capra. He wrote to me one day after having read a paper of mine entitled "The Integration of Form in Natural and in Theological Science" to say that I had been engaged there with the same problem he had been working with in particle and quantum theory. He had found it so difficult to express the way in which he found particles containing one another, as it were, within the structures of language of the Western type, that he had been forced to take over relational ways of thought from Hindu and Buddhist thought and also from Taoist thought, in order to develop appropriate modes of thought and speech for his scientific understanding of nature. In my reply I pointed out that the relational thinking of Hindu and Buddhist thought is not correlated with the empirical realities of nature, and indeed cannot be; so that relational thinking of that kind would hardly be appropriate for physics. Then I drew his attention to the concept of *perichoresis* in the Christian tradition. If we are to talk about particles somehow containing and interpenetrating one another, then why not use this way of thinking, for that is precisely the notion latent in *perichoresis* which Christian theology refined and developed to express the mutual coinherence of the Persons of the Holy Trinity? This perichoretic connection is essentially an onto-relational one which is, as I understood him, what Dr. Capra was after. Now granted that, as refined and exalted in the Holy Trinity, the perichoretic relation is not directly correlated with the physical world—how could it be?—nevertheless, it was reached through a movement of thought that took its rise from the empirico-theoretical ground of the incarnational activity of God within the spatio-temporal structures of our world, and it remains, indirectly through the level of the economic trinitarian relations, empirically correlated with that ground.

Hence it would not be surprising if a perichoretic relation, with appropriate and adequate change in relation to the nature of the subject-matter in the field, could be applied to the problem of quantum theory or of particle theory. And in fact that has been done with real success by Professor Christopher B. Kaiser in a work that is as yet unpublished. Here, then, we have an instance where Christian theology in its rigorous, scientific form can be of real help even to natural science, where it is concerned with the almost inexpressible, intricate, intelligible exchange-relations in the microphysical field.

Be that as it may, what I am concerned to do here is to indicate the kind of cross-play and cross-fertilization between theological and natural science, even when we have to do with a profound and difficult doctrine like that of the Holy Trinity. Certainly the stratified structure of theological inquiry and formulation—through which the understanding of Trinitarian relations in the One God is clarified and brought to expression in such a way that it constitutes the ultimate theological basis for the unifying and simplifying of all theology—is basically similar in its formal aspects to the stratified structure of a scientific system that yields an understanding of an objective relatedness in the universe as formulated through relativity theory, which for its part constitutes the unitary theoretic basis for the unification and simplification of physics. But this parallel is possible because both theological science and natural science operate within the same rational patterns of space and time, so that their inquiries—even if they move in different directions, as is demanded by the nature of their respective subject-matters—are bound to overlap; but this is also possible because, as we have seen, they share ideas that are basic to the operation and cognitive structure of each of them. Quite evidently theological science and natural science both have boundary conditions where they are conceptually open to one another, but they also have sufficient common ground, not least in the transition to a unitary outlook upon the universe, on which serious inter-disciplinary inquiry can be pursued with considerable advantage to both.

Several years ago, at my suggestion, the International Academy of Religious Sciences, held a seminar on the doctrine of the Trinity, in which we took our starting point from Karl Rahner's essay on the Trinity in *Mysterium Salutis* (1967). The seminar comprised theologians from the Roman Catholic, Orthodox, Reformed, Lutheran, Anglican, and Congregational traditions, who worked very hard for several days. We found ourselves steadily reaching a remarkable unity in the approaches of East and West, of

Evangelical and Catholic theology, in which the views of Rahner and Barth were brought together on a patristic basis. The results have been published in French and German journals. The lesson I take from that and hand on to you is this: when we pursue some theological theme on its own proper ground, but with the same kind of scientific rigor we use in natural science, and within the context in which dualist modes of thought are transcended, we achieve profound advance and agreement. That is, I believe, as it ought to be.

We are in a difficult transitional period, in which those of us who are middle-aged or older—in science, I am told, you are middle-aged when you are thirty!—find these new onto-relational ways of thought rather difficult, as they conflict with our habits of mind. But soon we shall have new generations of minds that will be at home or at ease in onto-relational thought, whether in theological or in natural science, for onto-relational thinking is only a refinement of our ordinary and natural modes of connection. The future thus seems to be full of promise and excitement. Certainly at no time for nearly a millennium and a half has the opportunity for genuine theology been greater, since the ground has been cleared in the most remarkable way of the old dualist and atomistic modes of thought that have plagued theology for centuries. It is, therefore, up to us as theologians to develop theology on its own proper ground in this scientific context, if only because this is the kind of theology needed to change the foundations of modern life and culture, and the kind of theology that can support the message of the Gospel to mankind, as, in touch with the advances of natural science, theology comes closer and closer to a real understanding of the creation as it came from the hand of God.

Index of Names

Al Ghazali, 54
Anselm of Canterbury, 80, 99–100, 151
Aquinas, Thomas, 79, 83
Arianism, 38, 42
Aristotle, 21, 25, 46, 49, 61, 64
Arius, 68
Athanasius, 53, 58, 60, 66–68, 76–78, 93, 117, 124, 151, 158
Athenagoras of Athens, 58
Augustine of Hippo, 61, 63, 99, 148

Bacon, Francis, 5, 51
Barth, Karl, 12, 67, 87–94, 143, 147, 178
Boethius, A. M. T. S., 173
Born, Max, 113
Brunner, Emil, 89
Buber, Martin, 149–50
Bukharin, N. I., 113
Bultmann, Rudolf, 18–19, 36

Calvin, John, 174
Capra, Fritjof, 175–76
Chalcedonian Definition of the Faith, 126–27
Clement of Alexandria, 58, 60
Cook, Alan, 103
Copernicus, 21, 83
Cyril of Alexandria, 50, 60, 158

Descartes, René, 21, 23–24

Eccles, Sir John, 4
Einstein, Albert, 3, 5, 7, 11, 23, 30–31, 35, 72, 91, 105, 112–14, 119, 127–28, 130, 145, 156, 162, 168–69, 171
Euclid, 92, 147
Eutyches, 118, 126

Faraday, Michael, 11
Fermat, P. de, 108

Galileo Galilei, 21, 23, 83
Gnosticism, 37–38, 42
Gödel, Kurt, 70
Gregory of Nazianzus, 158
Grosseteste, Robert, 54
Grotius, Hugo, 85
Gunton, Colin, 147

Hamilton, Sir William, 7
Hartt, Julian, 96
Heidegger, Martin, 42, 81
Herrmann, W., 23
Hume, David, 25

Jaki, Stanley L., 58, 101
Job, 130–31
John of Damascus, 66, 78–79

Kaiser, Christopher B., 176
Kant, Immanuel, 21, 23, 25–27, 84, 86, 162
Katsir, B., 12
Kuhn, Thomas S., 47

Laplace, P. S., 70
Leibniz, G. W., 81
Leo the Great, 61, 127
Lessing, G. E., 23
Locke, John, 23, 25, 76, 174
Lonergan, Bernard, 147
Lovell, Sir Bernard, 3–4, 140, 142

Mach, Ernst, 29, 35, 42–43
Mackinnon, Alastair, 131
Mascall, Eric L., 87
Maxwell, James Clerk, 7
Mercier, André, 134

Nestorius, 118, 126
Newton, Sir Isaac, 21, 23–24, 26, 68–71, 76, 83–85, 101
Nicene-Constantinopolitan Creed, 39, 118, 159–60

Pauli, W., 113
Philoponos, John, 54, 60–61, 127
Planck, Max, 42, 72
Plato, 21, 49, 61
Polanyi, Michael, 14, 59, 113–14, 141
Prigogine, Ilya, 12, 141
Przywara, Erich, 88
Pseudo-Cyril, 79
Pseudo-Dionysius, 78
Pythagoras, 116

Rahner, Karl, 177–78
Richard of St. Victor, 174
Ritschl, A., 27, 42

Schleiermacher, F. D. E., 27, 42
Schrödinger, E., 4
Scotus, John Duns, 174
Spinoza, B., 150

Tillich, Paul, 150

Weyl, Hermann, 3, 128
Wheeler, John Archibald, 4, 140